W9-AHA-079

The Reluctant Empath

BETY COMERFORD AND STEVE WILSON

Schiffer Publishing Ltd

4880 Lower Valley Road • Atglen, PA 19310

Other Schiffer Books by the Author:

Ghost and Shamanic Tales of True Hauntings
9780764341281 $16.99

Copyright © 2014 by Bety Comerford and Steve Wilsom

Library of Congress Control Number: 2014931878

All rights reserved. No part of this work may be reproduced or used in any form
or by any means—graphic, electronic, or mechanical, including photocopying
or information storage and retrieval systems—without written permission from
the publisher.

The scanning, uploading, and distribution of this book or any part thereof via
the Internet or via any other means without the permission of the publisher is
illegal and punishable by law. Please purchase only authorized editions and do
not participate in or encourage the electronic piracy of copyrighted materials.
"Schiffer," "Schiffer Publishing, Ltd. & Design," and the "Design of pen and
inkwell" are registered trademarks of Schiffer Publishing, Ltd.

Designed by Molly Shields
Cover designed by Justin Watkinson
Type set in NewBskvll BT

ISBN: 978-0-7643-4603-3
Printed in China

Published by Schiffer Publishing, Ltd.
4880 Lower Valley Road
Atglen, PA 19310
Phone: (610) 593-1777; Fax: (610) 593-2002
E-mail: Info@schifferbooks.com

For our complete selection of fine books on this and related subjects, please visit
our website at www.schifferbooks.com. You may also write for a free catalog.

This book may be purchased from the publisher. Please try your bookstore first.

We are always looking for people to write books on new and related subjects. If
you have an idea for a book, please contact us at proposals@schifferbooks.com

Schiffer Publishing's titles are available at special discounts for bulk purchases
for sales promotions or premiums. Special editions, including personalized
covers, corporate imprints, and excerpts can be created in large quantities for
special needs. For more information, contact the publisher.

Front cover image: Sad young woman and rain drops ©
Bigedhar. Courtesy www.bigstockphoto.com.

*We can't solve problems by
using the same kind of thinking
we used when we created them.*
—Albert Einstein

About the Authors

Bety Comerford and Steve Wilson

Bety Comerford and Steve Wilson are both shamanic healers and empaths who have helped many people understand their empathic gifts and heal those parts of themselves that keep them from living a fulfilling life.

Bety is a third generation medium and psychic. She is the author of *Ghost and Shamanic Tales of True Hauntings*.

Steve is a Spiritualist Minister and teaches shamanism at his spiritual center, The Sacred Healing Grove, www.sacredhealinggrove.com, located in Mason, New Hampshire.

Dedication

From Bety

To Larry, who allows me to walk in my truth every day. To Mamacita, whose smile lights up the world. To all the Alex's of the world, both male and female, who have suffered as empaths. To Diane, JoAnn, and Debbie, who never laughed at this empath. To the gang at the yurt who is our second family. To OT, Gloria, Jacqui, and Sasha who have always believed. And to Steve, spiritual teacher, friend, and fellow traveler on this always-amazing path.

From Steve Wilson

To my son, Steve, my daughter, Nichoal, and their better halfs, Becky and Jeremy, who push me to be who I am. To Tristin, Tavian, and Lila, to whom I want to leave a better world. To my mom, sisters, and brother, for putting up with my craziness. To my father, who was the strongest man I ever knew. To Lisa, Alley, and Drew, who make me smile when I forget. To Michelle Hanson, Arlene Dorischild, Rev. Trish, Rev. Al, Rev. Betsy, who were there at the right times of my life. To John Perkins, Lyn Roberts, and Bill Pfeiffer, inspirational teachers who have made me go "aha!" more times than I can remember. To the Aquarius Sanctuary, the National Spiritualist Alliance, the Church in the Wyldewood, the peeps at the yurt and, lastly to Bety, my spiritual sister through many lives and many adventures.

Contents

INTRODUCTION...8

CHAPTER 1: Your Words Don't Match Your Heart.............10

What happens when a person's true intentions don't match their words? An an empath, you feel the difference...you feel the projected energy of the other person. You begin to learn discernment – what is true and what isn't.

CHAPTER 2: Protection, Protection, Protection.................20

Everyone is always trying to protect themselves from the Other Side and from each other. The only protection that never fails is no fear and the ability to move energy.

CHAPTER 3: Better to Keep Quiet.................................32

Everyone wants to fit in, including an empath. But as you try to understand your gift, you tell your stories to others who don't understand or they ridicule you. You learn very quickly to keep quiet. Why, when the truth of what you are seeking lies in tapping into the vibrational energy of love?

CHAPTER 4: Why do I Get All the Bad Stuff?..................41

Much of what is taught in the New Age Community does not address the deep healing necessary to face anything and everything that comes at you. When the energy turns bad, it all falls apart. Why? How does energy work and can you be strong when the energy does turn bad?

CHAPTER 5: It Lasts Forever.....................................51

Every thought, every emotion, every trauma that a human being has experienced since the beginning of time is out there in the ethers that surround us. As an empath, you have the responsibility of watching what you're putting out there because other empaths are feeling it. How can you use these situations as a powerful healing tool?

CHAPTER 6: It Is What It Is...58

You can drive yourself crazy trying to figure out why you are feeling what you are feeling and whether it has a particular meaning. Many times it means nothing; it's just an experience of energy, which adds to the "tool box" of knowledge for you to learn how energy works.

CHAPTER 7: Simultaneous Time..70

An empath can feel and access the past, present, and future, sometimes all at the same time. Why does this happen and how can you deal with such a situation?

CHAPTER 8: This Stuff Really Works................................79

Manifesting, casting spells, throwing energy balls, projecting one's energy – it all works. However, they each have their own lessons and their own responsibilities. Then there's a little matter known as instant karma…

CHAPTER 9: Manifestation 101.......................................88

An empath's guide to manifesting responsibly.

CHAPTER 10: It's All a Test...94

Many times you will experience things that test your fears: a vision, a dream, a particularly unnerving situation. It is all part of learning how you and others use their energy. As you learn to overcome your fears, more psychic gifts and abilities are given that allows you to more fully step onto your path.

CHAPTER 11: Energy Evolution...100

As you learn and surrender to your lessons, your
personal vibration and abilities increase. You are
evolving to your highest potential and in that evolution
are able to help others.

CHAPTER 12: We Are a Gift to Each Other.....................................105

As you evolve, you will learn the gift of service to others
who have forgotten their own paths. It is a difficult
world out there, but there is a way to get through it.
This is the role of the empath: to learn the way and
then teach others.

AFTERWORD...112

Introduction

What is an empath? A simple explanation is that an empath is a "human sponge." It's someone who feels what everyone else is feeling. They instantly know when someone is having a bad day, or if someone is lying to them, even if they don't quite understand how they know these things. It's someone who has a difficult time in malls or in crowded streets (especially around the holidays) because they feel bombarded by so many differing emotions coming at them from all sides. An empath is also someone who picks up the emotions of the dead. Ghosts are the spirits of people who have not crossed into the Light because they are still hanging onto heavy human emotions, such as grief, hatred, sadness, guilt, and others. An empath feels not only these oppressive emotions from the living, but from the dead as well. Many have no idea what to do with these feelings. They see this not as a gift, but as a curse. Some medicate themselves, some drink, some turn off emotionally so they don't have to feel anything anymore.

However, there is another way to look at what being an empath is all about. Energy is made up of different vibrations. For example, the energy of depression is of a lower vibration because of its density. You "feel heavy" when depressed. The energy of love is the complete opposite. That euphoric feeling of love is of a much lighter vibration. You "feel light" when you're in love.

What if you realized that instead of thinking of empathy as a curse, you instead were taught to see it as a wonderful gift?

Most books about empathy talk about protecting yourself: clearing yourself constantly of the energies you're feeling. But what if we were to tell you to stop clearing? To stop protecting? To allow yourself to willingly feel everything you're feeling? Science tells us that energy cannot be destroyed. But its vibration can be changed. And that's where you come in.

Imagine not only feeling every thought and every emotion a person has, whether living or dead, but understanding that at any given moment in your life, past, present, and future are colliding all at once. Imagine everything that you've ever thought and felt, whether it be in this life or another life, coming back to you for you to look at because the energy of that experience is being reflected by whatever you're now thinking or feeling. Imagine suddenly discovering that your entire life has been mapped out and you are having visions of that planning just to teach you what it means to be an empath.

We grew up as empaths. We felt everything. And yes, we too felt at times that it was a burden, a curse. But as we grew older and started on our respective spiritual paths, we began to learn the dynamics of what it truly meant to be an empath. It was more than just feeling emotions.

The true gift of the empath is to change the energy of those emotions, not just your own, but those of others around you.

It's learning how to put a higher vibrational energy into a lower vibrational energy and feel it lighten up. It's bringing light into a dark place, even if that dark place is inside your own soul.

We are both shamanic healers. The majority of the clients in our private practices come to us because they feel too much, or, burdened by the weight of too much emotion, have shut down and don't feel anything at all. Neither is acceptable to leading a healthy, fulfilling life.

When we sat down to discuss what kind of book to write as a follow-up to *Ghost and Shamanic Tales of True Hauntings*, we thought a book about empathy would be a useful tool. So many people don't know what to do with these gifts. Many of our children are being given drugs because they feel too much and are winding up as emotionless robots.

This, therefore, is the story of Alex, a person who fought tooth and nail against the idea that he was an empath. Yet, in the fight and struggle, he learned the truth of who he was, what others were, and who they were becoming. He learned why the world was designed the way it was.

Each chapter will break down different aspects of what it is to be an empath. You will experience what Alex experienced. Hopefully, you too will have gone through some of the events Alex experienced. You will discover that many were reluctant at first to embrace these gifts. You'll learn about simultaneous time, how your life is mapped out (yes, free will does play into it, but we will explain free will in a way you may not be expecting), and more. By the end of this book, you will know that, far from being a curse, empathy is truly a wonderful and awesome gift.

Although each word we've written is true, some of these experiences may be alien to you. But some may strike a chord because you've lived through it, or knew or now know people going through it. Know that it is all part of a bigger journey. It is a journey towards acceptance, not only of other human beings, but more importantly, of yourself.

—Bety Comerford and Steve Wilson

1

Your Words Don't Match Your Heart

What happens when a person's true intentions don't match their words? An an empath, you feel the difference...you feel the projected energy of the other person. You begin to learn discernment – what is true and what isn't.

Children are born into this world as tiny bundles of love and innocence. It is difficult not to hold a newborn child and be awed by the sense of love they elicit in our hearts or the fierce sense of protectiveness we feel towards such an innocent little being.

It is the life experiences this little child will live through that will begin the process of losing sight of who they really are. Such is the difficult journey of the empath. As they grow, they will experience every human emotion there is to experience. The difference between their experiences and those of others is that, as an empath, they will feel these emotions so deeply, so acutely, that they can be easily overwhelmed by it all.

So why go through this? Because of the greater opportunities these experiences will give the empathic child to learn the nuances of energy and how they react to that energy.

As it is with most empathic children, they tend to be born into less-than-ideal situations. It's not that they're not loved by their parents. On the contrary, they learn early on how the love they receive from their mothers and fathers feel. It's wonderful and warm and nurturing and they crave to be surrounded by that love at all times. Why? Because love has a high energetic vibration to it.

The ideal situation for an empath is to live in a world where all they feel is that energy of a higher vibration. Unfortunately, as they begin to live their lives, that need for high vibrational energy has the potential to manifest itself as neediness. They recognize what that energy feels like and they seek to recapture it as often as they can, any way they can.

This was the journey of Alex. Coming into this world, he had all the typical physical needs and wants of every child: the need for food, for clothing, for warmth. But, like any empathic child, he was different. Oh, he looked like any rambunctious, mischievous little boy. However, below the surface, he harbored a sharp emotional sensitivity. He had the constant need to be held, yet at the same time, he also had the need to be left alone. At first, this constant ebb and flow of emotional needs and wants didn't make sense to him. Why did he feel the overwhelming desire to be held while, at the same time, the great need to be alone? His reactions always stemmed from the emotional context of his environment – a trigger that would cause him to seek a place of safety within himself.

At a young age, Alex found himself drawn to animals and vice versa. He perceived, even if he didn't quite understand it at the time, that their love, their comfort, and their attentiveness provided him with that place of safety he craved.

Whenever he wandered into his backyard and stood in the presence of the large, majestic oak trees, the silence of the grass and the flowers and the trees themselves provided a sanctuary for him. He felt, on a deep, subconscious level, their unconditional and non-judgmental love. It wasn't until he grew older that he realized that, unlike humans, trees and nature were happy being trees and nature. They didn't have the drive or the need to be something other than what they were. However, as a young boy, all he felt was the loving, calming energy emanating from these guardians of the forest.

It wasn't until he became aware of his interactions with those humans in his everyday life that he began to realize just how different he was. In the beginning, his human interaction was limited to his parents and relatives. They were all very loving and caring, projecting a sense of serenity whenever he was present. However, the longer he was in their presence, the more he began to perceive an underlying current that didn't feel entirely comfortable. He would look to their faces and see smiles and laughter, yet within his own physical body, he felt heavy and uneasy.

Family gatherings and holidays were especially difficult for Alex. It was perplexing to see his siblings deal with the natural stresses that accompanied large family gatherings while he felt overwhelmed by the energy of it all. For reasons he could not understand, the heaviness and discomfort would grow until he had no choice but to escape back to the inner world of his pets and plants, where he felt safe and serene and where his body could return to a state of well-being.

This strange experience of seeing one thing, yet experiencing another was brought home to him when he was about four years old. It was a cold autumn day, the rain tapping against the windowpane of the living-room windows. Unlike most children, who only saw rain as a hindrance to playing outside, Alex found the light pattering of the rain comforting. He knew the water that fell from the skies nourished his beloved trees and plants, and he felt their joy as the rain hit their upturned leaves and quenched their thirst.

However, he could never share this with his mother. Instinctually, despite his young age, there were some things he knew not to share with anyone. So, like all the children in the neighborhood on that rainy day, he sat inside on the living-room floor, entertaining himself with his collection of toy soldiers.

Off in the distance, he heard the doorbell ring. A moment later, his mother and their next-door neighbor, Patty, entered the living room and sat on the couch near to where he was quietly playing. Patty often stopped by to share a cup of coffee and gossip, though it struck him as strange that she would come out on such a raw, blustery day. His curiosity peaked; he glanced up at her out of the corner of his eye. There was an excitement in her eyes while, at the same time, her mouth was pinched, as though she were trying to hold back tears of sadness.

Sometimes it was good to be four years old. Adults usually ignored his presence and he was able to find out all sorts of interesting information. This day was no different. While he made sure not to make any noise and call unwanted attention to himself, he listened as Patty recounted, in great detail, the troubles another neighborhood family was experiencing.

"He was cheating on her with his secretary. Can you imagine!" Patty exclaimed. "Of course, she's filing for divorce."

"That's terrible," Alex's mother murmured, shaking her head in commiseration.

"They're going to have to sell the house. The kids are heartbroken because they can't keep the pets. Most apartments won't let you bring in a dog and a cat. What an absolute disaster. And all because of his wandering eye. You just can't trust anyone these days, including your own husband it seems."

Watching Patty surreptitiously from beneath his brow, he noticed her face awash with sympathy as she sipped her coffee. However, to his amazement, Alex knew the pitying look Patty was expressing was completely false. He didn't know how he knew, but as sure as he could feel the plastic of the toy soldiers in his hands, he knew that rather than pity the family she was talking about, Patty was taking pleasure in their disaster. He studied her face, trying to discern how he could know this. Her facial expression and the tone of her voice gave nothing away. Yet he felt the truth of her emotions deep in his belly and in his heart, so much so that it was causing actual pain and discomfort.

The same situation presented itself over and over to Alex. Instead of Patty, it became aunts and uncles, cousins, friends. Somehow he knew when they were being false, though he couldn't understand how he knew this.

He was too young and too inexperienced to comprehend that the energy of the statement and the energy of the intention weren't matching up. Patty's intention towards the family was one of smug superiority. She felt better about herself and her family as she watched the other family's world fall apart. She kept such a strict eye on her husband, she knew he'd never cheat on her. She simply wouldn't permit it. Yet she couldn't present the truth of how she was feeling to those around her. So she hid behind an untrue façade.

It wasn't long before Alex's exploration of the world around him expanded outside the four walls of his home into the world of friendships. There was an excitement that beyond the environs of his house, there was much to experience. What he didn't know, in his naive enthusiasm, was that there were also painful lessons waiting to be learned as well.

When he was five years old, a family with three brothers moved into his neighborhood. One day he noticed they had a shiny rock they were playing with. It was so sparkly and pretty, he felt drawn to that rock and wanted it desperately. It seemed to emanate an energy, a light, something that reminded him of his dealings with his pets and plant life.

In the course of trying to get the rock, he found himself doing all he could to fit into the little group of newfound friends. Whatever they wanted, he would do. If they asked him to climb the highest tree, he'd do it, despite his fear of heights. If they wanted him to throw a rock at a passing car, he'd do it, despite knowing it was wrong. He noticed that whenever they egged him on to do something and he did it, they laughed and giggled. Being a friendly, sweet boy, his natural reaction was one of joy. Surely they'll give me the rock, he thought to himself, because I'm bringing them so much love and happiness. Look at the way they laugh and smile whenever I'm around.

This lesson would continue.

As the start of the school year approached, he found himself excited, yet nervous at the same time. What will it be like riding the bus? Who will be there? Will the kids like me? But Alex was a naturally curious child and his adventuresome curiosity pushed these fears away.

The first day of school arrived. Climbing onto the big, yellow bus, he slid into a seat halfway down the aisle. The bus was half full of jabbering students and, although he didn't know anyone, he was still excited about this big step in his life. It wasn't long before he was surrounded by a group of older boys who'd been sitting at the back of the bus. He was asked questions he had no answers for, yet he gamely tried to answer them to the best of his ability from a place of innocence and an innate understanding that words have the power to elicit responses that made him feel good physically.

Answering the questions, he noticed the boys laughed and giggled. Just as he'd done with the three brothers, he interpreted their reaction to his words with joy and happiness. He was entertaining them, so naturally they must like him.

This went on every day on the bus ride to and from school. One day, he casually shared his experiences with his mother, telling her how much the older kids liked him and recounting the questions they asked. The unexpected look of horror on her face shot through young Alex's heart like a dagger.

"Alex," she replied compassionately, "these boys are not your friends. They're picking on you and laughing at your expense."

"What do you mean?" he asked, his eyes brimming with bewilderment.

Not wanting to hurt him, his mother held back from responding. Yet, although she spoke no words, Alex immediately felt the energy of his mother's concern and her worry of how easy it was for others to take advantage of her sensitive son. It left him perplexed. How could his mother have such a different response than what the boys on the bus were having? Her emotions and feelings at that moment did not match up to the love and joy he thought the boys were experiencing whenever they heard his answers to the questions they asked him.

What was going on?

In that moment, Alex felt cold. And heavy. And upset that he did not understand.

The next day on the bus, he went in with a different perspective. He climbed on the bus with his guard up. His natural curiosity and openness was gone, replaced by his mother's concerns and worries. Immediately, the questions were different that day. They were more hurtful. The boys took on a more menacing, bullying air. The feelings of euphoria he'd once felt from eliciting laughter from these boys was completely gone. The more they made fun of him, the heavier and weaker he became. It was as though they were taking from him the very thing he held so dear – his connection to love. He began to realize, just as he'd done with Patty and his family, that the words and facial expressions were not matching up to the energetic intent. His innocence had kept him protected from reality.

The seeds of these experiences began to grow. Not only was Alex experiencing a different context in his dealings with people visually, but physically he was starting to notice how his body reacted to the inconsistency of what people were saying and how he felt when he heard their words. He couldn't yet comprehend why animals and nature brought him so much comfort and joy emotionally and physically, becoming better and more reliable friends than the people he encountered in his everyday life.

As these situations continued, Alex felt different because of his empathic ability. Empaths feel things so deeply; many times it goes beyond words, beyond what can be adequately described, because what they feel is experienced on such an intensely physical level.

Alex's new paradigm became the necessity of keeping himself safe at all times. In order to feel safe, he needed to do his best not to stand out. He needed and wanted to fit in and be like all his friends and siblings.

This is called "bargaining." So many people who want to fit in begin to bargain the true core of who they are away. Many will become the clown. If I make people laugh, I'll fit in and they'll like me. The more you start to become a person who you think people will like, the more you start to exist outside yourself. You don't begin to get a sense of who you are because there's always this need to get energy – to get that love, that acceptance. At first, that energy feels good. Hey, they like me! I'm part of the group. They're accepting me.

Unfortunately, as Alex painfully found out, despite all he did to try to fit in with both the brothers and the boys on the bus, instead of accepting his friendship, they laughed at him. They realized how much they were enjoying the feeling of mastery they had over Alex. Whatever they told him to do, he would do. Instead of seeing it as his attempt to fit in, they saw him as their own personal door mat. Their words of friendship were not matching their intention. The vibration of the energy began to lower. Now, instead of feeling good whenever he was with these boys, Alex began to feel the opposite.

How many of us have been in similar situations? How many of us have fallen into the trap of thinking: If I keep giving, they'll eventually accept me, or like me, or even love me. There's a lot of giving going on. Just not a lot of getting back. How many times in our lives have we found ourselves standing in the presence of someone and a heaviness overcomes us – as if we're being drained of our very vital life force? These are the experiences of an empath. In our need or our desire to fit in, we find ourselves bargaining ourselves away. We're giving away the core of who we really are so we can continue to feel love, to feel acceptance. But, like Alex, we eventually find out that it doesn't last. Because false things never do last.

By the time an empath comes into their teenage years, they do one of two things: they continue to bargain themselves away, or they turn away from people, sometimes their own families, because they know something is off and they can't take feeling that lower energy anymore, even if they don't quite understand why. Some may retreat into themselves.

In the case of Alex, he found himself reverting to the only world he ever felt safe within his childhood: that of the world of nature. In nature, where a tree is happy being a tree or a squirrel is happy being a squirrel, Alex felt non-judgmental love. It was in his connection to nature where he began to learn how the physical world functioned in an energetic way.

Everything on this earth has a vibration, be it the trees, stones, animals, or people. When a child feels love from their parents, they bask in it. They enjoy it because it feels good. However, when parents don't give a child love, the child quickly learns how awful the loss of that energy feels. Being empathic, these children will feel the loss of that energy even more acutely. So what do they do? They start to do things to attract attention – to attract the energy of love to themselves.

In fact, the bullies on the bus and the three brothers in Alex's life were doing the same. As the boys reveled in the reaction they were eliciting from Alex, they were actually receiving his energy. Alex was giving his energy away in an attempt to be liked and accepted and they were taking it. The more he gave, the more they took. However, once Alex put his guard up and cut off his energy from them, the boys on the bus began to bully and taunt him in an attempt to recapture the energy he'd once so freely provided. The boys never would have understood what they were doing. But somewhere in their subconscious they would have felt the loss of Alex's energy and would resort to whatever they had to do to recapture it, strengthening themselves and weakening him.

Emotions too have a vibration – an energy that can be physically felt. It is believed in many cultures that this vibration is the life force that is present in all things. It has many names: "prana" in Vedantic philosophy, "chi" in

China, "wind horse" in Native American lore, the "Holy Spirit" in Christian circles. Even the movies have capitalized on this emotional vibration, calling it "The Force" in the popular *Star Wars* films. The natural world works flawlessly – nothing is other than what it is – the vibration of its life force perfect in every way. This was why Alex felt so safe when surrounded by animals and trees and stones. It was as if a mutual acceptance was taking place. He accepted and respected nature for what it was and vice versa.

In the world of human beings, the energy of this life force is expressed as thought, deed, or an emotion. As we can see by watching the nightly news, these thoughts, deeds, and emotions do not work as flawlessly as the energy of nature. Humans do not easily accept each other for who he or she is. There is a constant battle to impose thoughts and deeds and emotions on others. It is this miasma of dysfunctional energy that an empath is bombarded with constantly.

Yet this energy, which is a gift to all things, is also the lesson of the empath. How else will you fit into the world without experiencing how energy is used? How will you learn without going through, on a physical level, when energy feels good and when it doesn't? How will you grow if you don't question the meanings of words, of facial expressions, of probing the very actions of those around you?

When someone is angry, you certainly feel the energy of that. You also feel when someone is happy or depressed. Love itself has an energy that anyone who has ever felt love can testify to. Being in love makes you feel as though you can walk on air. Being in love or feeling love from someone else makes time seem to fly by. That energy feels really good, which is why human beings spend their whole lives trying to find or keep love.

Alex's way to find solace was in nature. Others may start to create a fantasy world for themselves where they don't have to deal with other people's emotions. They may immerse themselves in books, or art, or music – anything that will elicit and switch them back to that feeling of love and acceptance, of feeling better than what they normally feel, of feeling good in their own body. This is because somewhere along the way, although they may not entirely grasp how or why, being around humans doesn't always feel comfortable. Many times the empath will first feel this on a physical level. There may be a pain in the stomach or in the chest, or a sudden uneasy feeling that is unexplainable. Not until you begin to mentally comprehend that the intention of a person doesn't always match up with their words will you feel the energy of an untruth that another person. And when you do, it doesn't feel good at all.

Why does this happen? Because truth itself has a vibration of energy. It's a higher intention and vibrates at a higher frequency. When a person's words match their truthful intention, you will feel good because it does feel good. Higher vibrations always feel good. How do we know this? Because your innate expectations of your energetic experience have been met. In that moment, the vibration that has been gifted to you has filled you. No discomfort is evident. It is the same feeling you get when you are in that serene space of nature, or your fantasy world, or any other place where the energy or vibration resides in truth.

Think about this for a moment. How do you feel when you are depressed or sad? You feel heavy because these emotions spin at a lower frequency. They weigh you down, make you feel as though you're walking through sludge. Time seems to drag on forever. Now think about those moments when you've heard someone tell you they love you, yet somewhere inside your heart, you know they're not being truthful with you. How do you know this? Because it just doesn't feel right. It feels off. No matter how many times you try to convince yourself otherwise, there's still that tiny doubt in the back of your head that knows the truth. How? Because the energy of an untruth is coming at you at a lower vibration. You may not understand the mechanics of it, but you will feel it.

You may be thinking, what makes an empath different? Doesn't everyone feel when someone is lying? Doesn't everyone feel what we're talking about in this book? Aren't all human beings, to some extent, empathic? Yes, they are. But there are degrees of empathy. Many people live in their heads. They see the world through logic and squeeze everything that happens through the tube of rational reasoning. However, there are people, and these are the ones we address here, who feel things so deeply, so intensely, on a physical level, that logic and rational reasoning don't work. They don't explain why an empath feels sick when in a crowd. They don't explain how or why an empath is so sensitive. They are aware of the subtle nuances of energy or the shifts that happen in an instant that pass most people by.

Because of your ability to feel emotions on such a deep level, you will be placed into unique situations to understand why your physical experience is so uncomfortable. These opportunities become your driving force to understand why you are uncomfortable. You can only hide from life's realities for so long – especially when all things leave energetic cobwebs that you find yourself walking into continuously. Words, deeds, actions, lack of actions, lack of words: all these things wield an energy that we've come to this world to understand. As an empath, you will feel the ramifications of these things, the truth of these things. And you begin to clamor for the understanding of these things.

So what do you do about it? Do you hide? Do you run? Do you shut yourself off? Do you force yourself to feel or not feel? As in nature, you will begin to realize there is a balancing factor or force to the life and the journey of every human being.

We are here to feel, to experience, to learn. That's what being a human being is all about. Hopefully, at some point, you will start to look at yourself and learn these things. You will realize that all your experiences are serving to teach you. Rather than fight what comes at you, you can begin to embrace these situations and see the experiences for what they are. They're happening because, as an empath, you have a job to do. But you have to lay down the foundations. Just as a house needs its foundations to stand against the harshest weather conditions, you too need a foundation to withstand all that the world throws at you. Then, rather than seeing your abilities as a curse, you will start to see them as a gift. All that you will experience will serve as building blocks that assist you in learning about energy, not only yours, but others' as well. As we said in our introduction, physics tell us that energy cannot be destroyed. But its vibration can be changed. As an empath, that is what you're here to do.

The more you embrace your role, the more you can meet your lessons head-on and not become overwhelmed by them. It helps to know that as you go through these lessons, you are not alone by any means. Millions are going through this.

We ourselves have gone through this throughout our lives. Frankly, we had no choice; and neither do you. Life doesn't stop because you don't want to deal with being an empath. In fact, you'll find that certain situations, or certain types of people, reoccur over and over in your life. Why? Because they're there to teach you. Until you "get it right," they'll continue popping up in your life, giving you further opportunities to learn the lesson that needs to be learned. So pay attention to all that happens to you. There's probably a lesson in there somewhere for you to look at, absorb its ramifications, and from there to move forward.

ENERGETIC SAFETY

It's important to find a place of energetic safety. What is energetic safety? Whether its nature or something created, it's a space of no energetic intention. Music, stones, neutral colors, the sound of gentle flowing water can bring that calmness that you, as an empath, crave. The need to cleanse your body is no different than needing to cleanse your palate when tasting wine.

In the beginning, it will be difficult for you to quantify your experience when so many energies have become part of your physical experience, even to the point of finding their way into your physical body in the form of headaches, stomach ailments, etc. It is not hard to look around and see how many people are on overload, especially children, or those who have turned to drugs, alcohol, or other addictive habits in an effort to deal with the explosion of emotion they are experiencing. It's important to create a neutral zone where you (and they) can begin to find your own sense of self and renewal in order to meet each day and, at the same time, calmly try to come to an understanding of what energy is all about.

Therefore, create a space of energy curiosity that has no intention. A corner in a yard or room, a favorite stone, beautiful flowers, perhaps small bushes or trees, maybe in the shape of a circle, where an empathic child or adult can find themselves in their own solitude with things that bring comfort. A quiet space where you can be within yourself. It will teach you how to make a serene, safe place where you can retreat, and where you can begin to detach from the feeling of being overwhelmed by the energy of others. It often helps to bring nature into a room.

This doesn't mean to detach from the world. It's a resting place to help come back to a sense of energetic calmness. To be in the world, but not of it.

If you can find a place of energetic calmness, you can begin to realize you have choices – that these energies you experience on a daily basis do not have to be so overwhelming. You can begin to understand, within your safety zone, that you also have a responsibility in your own dealings and interactions with others regarding how they put forth their own energies. If you can perceive and project calmness into a world that makes others feel uncomfortable, this is the first step on the journey and understanding of the gifts an empath is born with.

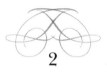

2

Protection, Protection, Protection

Everyone is always trying to protect themselves from the Other Side and from each other. The only protection that never fails is no fear and the ability to move energy.

The good news about being an empath is that you feel everything. The bad news about being an empath is that you feel everything.

As a young boy, already feeling overwhelmed by the emotions of others, Alex began to come up with various abilities to make himself feel safe. Although he didn't quite understand what he was experiencing yet, he did know it wasn't easy being in this world. Large gatherings of people felt uncomfortable to him; family gatherings had their own challenges. Unfortunately, more and more of his places of safety were beginning to fray and fall away.

His reaction to outside forces, the dysfunctions of others, were weighing him down. His own inability to understand what he was experiencing was building up in his physical body. He was beginning to find himself residing in a world of fear – a fear of interacting, a fear of having to be present in the dealings of others. As he tried to come up with ways to deal with these fears, the lesson of protection began to unfold.

If he hid in his safe place, he knew he was protected from all those things that made him feel uncomfortable. But in the infinite wisdom of parents who understand a child cannot hide away from the world forever, he was dragged kicking and screaming to places he knew would make his body ache and his head swoon and his heart hurt from the interaction with others.

There must be a way to get through this, he thought to himself. Maybe if I'm mean, they'll go away. Maybe if I act crazy, they'll leave me alone.

Ready to Write a Book?

We're always seeking authors for a wide variety of topics. This is your opportunity to shine! See our website to view an extensive list of our titles. If this idea appeals to you, we'd love to hear from you. Review our book submission guidelines at our website by clicking on the "Submit a Book Proposal" link. Then email your proposal and ideas to **proposals@schifferbooks.com** or write to the attention of **Acquisitions** at the address below. You can also call 610-593-1777 to make an appointment to speak with an editor.

Ⓢ Schiffer Publishing

has books covering a wide variety of interests including:

Antiques, Collectibles, & The Arts

• Advertising • Automobilia • Black Collectibles • Breweriana • Ceramics • Clocks • Corkscrews • Decoys • Dolls • Fine Art • Folk Art • Furniture • Graphic Art • Holidays • Hunting • Jewelry • Kitchen • Lighting • Leatherwork • Metalware • Native American Crafts • Nautical • Pinball • Quilts • Rugs • Sports • Teddy Bears • Telephones • Textiles • Toys • Video Games • Vintage Fashion • Watches • Writing Instruments and more.

Design, Lifestyle, & D-I-Y

• Architecture • Astrology • Counter Culture • Culinary Arts • Erotica • Interior Design • Kitchens and Baths • Landscaping • Numerology • Paranormal • Pin-Ups • Pop Art • Tarot • Tattooing • Textile Design • UFOs • Witchcraft • Basketry • Beads & Jewelry Making • Carving • Furniture Making • Gourds • Home & Garden • Metalwork • Modeling • Pyrography • Sculpture • Textiles • Weaving • Wood Turning • Tools and more.

Military, Aviation, & Automotive History

• WWI & WWII Armor/Aviation: German • U.S. • British • Russian • the Jet Age • Unit Biographies and Autobiographies • Edged Weapons • Firearms • Uniforms and more.

Maritime

• Seamanship • Navigation • Ship Management • Towing • Transportation • Boats & Boat Building • Medical • Legal and more.

Regional

• History • Children's Books • Architecture • Photography • Landscaping • Paranormal • Souvenir • Guidebooks • Cooking and more.

To learn more, go to www.schifferbooks.com
Call 610-593-1777, 8:30a.m.-5:30 p.m. EST
or write to 4880 Lower Valley Road
Atglen, PA 19310 USA
and ask for a free catalog(s).

In the UK and Europe contact
Bushwood Books at 44 (0) 20 8392-8585
info@bushwoodbooks.co.uk

Maybe if I'm quiet, they won't notice me. In a desperate attempt to make himself feel safe, all these behaviors became who he was.

With each energetic projection an empath makes, truth will somehow find its way into each thing that they do. As Alex's "acting out" in energy slowly became who he was, he found the energy he was drawing to himself actually made him feel worse. There is a saying that "like energy attracts like energy." Alex discovered the accuracy of this statement the hard way. The more he tried to repel the uncomfortable energy swirling around him, the more he attracted it to himself. The quest began to find whatever means possible to protect himself from feeling these heavy and negative energies.

As he grew older, Alex found himself looking into religion. What is prayer? Could this be his answer? Could this be the thing that made him feel better? But, just as in other moments in his life, when he'd found himself experiencing a situation where the words didn't match the intention, the same circumstances occurred in church where the energies didn't match up to the message preached. Those who prayed the hardest in church were the ones who, once the church service was over, picked on him the most.

So he dug deeper.

Maybe he wasn't praying correctly. Maybe he needed to try harder. He prayed fervently to find that thing, that magic object, that would bring him solace and love – anything that would make his journey easier to bear. How can this protect me? How can this keep me safe? That was his prayer. His mantra. He repeated the prayers over and over again, yet the discomfort he faced in his physical body continued.

He searched more.

He once again found himself turning back to nature. Maybe this was where his answer was. Maybe his protection lay in the stones. In the trees. He found himself drawn to books that spoke of the old ways – the ways of the Native Americans, the Druids. He read about the customs of the old cultures, poured over superstitions, studied all manner of thought processes that had to do with keeping one safe from the heaviness, the depression, the physical aches and pains stemming from the weight of the negative emotions he was picking up from the world around him. These experiences were beginning to take on a life of their own.

He still hadn't realized that the thoughts and feelings of everyone were beginning to manifest within him deeper and deeper fears. It was as if the very mental process of every living human being was speaking to him intrinsically at every twist and turn in his life.

Taking tests in school became a nightmare. Anxious of having to be present and physically feel the clamor and chaos of all the mental mishmash of thoughts from his fellow students, he found it impossible to concentrate. His grades began to suffer.

Then one day, quite by accident, he found a piece of the puzzle.

Walking through the woods behind his house, he absently picked up a stone that caught his eye. As he turned the stone over and over in his hand, he felt a curious sensation in his body, as if his very feet were connecting to the earth. Every uncomfortable feeling and emotion he'd been carrying around inside suddenly began to flow out the bottom of his feet into the ground. The more he felt the energy move out of him, the more clear-headed and physically better he felt. He stood in the middle of the forest path in wonderment. What had he just experienced? What was this moment of clarity? Was this the opportunity he'd been searching for that helped all the negativity he'd been building up in his body wash away?

His curiosity brought him back to exploring the different ways, over the centuries, that humanity had used to protect themselves against things they couldn't see or understand.

One day, by sheer luck, he was in the school library when he found a book that spoke of the evil eye and curses and spell casting. He read about the gypsies and their belief system, the old pagan beliefs, anything that spoke of this energy that he couldn't seem to get a handle on. His own fears and anxieties continued to grow and deepen. Was he cursed? Was he being hit with the evil eye? Was it trickery or the negativity of dark forces that were beginning to find their way into his life?

He began to experiment with the different protection modalities he read about. Thanks to his experience in his backyard, he knew that if he held certain stones, they would wash him clean of these energies, as if a spigot were opening up on the soles of his feet, flushing out those uncomfortable energies into the earth. To his dismay, however, he discovered the feeling of lightness would only last a little while before the heavy energies inevitably built up again. Obviously more was needed. But what?

Alex found himself reading about the wizards of old – of Merlin in particular. He read how the great old wizard was able to cast walls in front of him that nothing could penetrate. He immersed himself in esoteric studies of magic and alchemy. He tried to cast these metaphysical walls, these invisible barriers to keep all that bothered him out. To his surprise, he found he was able to do it. But each time he wielded his power to create something to keep him safe, something bigger came along and cast him back to scrambling about for another protection technique.

During this time, Alex realized, with a sinking feeling in his belly, that the emotions he was coming in contact with were not just coming at him from the living. Now they were coming at him from the Other Side and entering his dream time.

He experienced nightmares – all manner of creatures coming to him while he slept, telling him things, taking him places that, when he awoke, left him exhausted and confused. He looked for ways to shut down this intrusion. Who were these spirits that invaded his dreams? Were they benevolent? Were they evil? Did they have their own agenda, using him for their own ends?

He'd read about spirits that interacted with the living. Now, not only was he sensing emotions from those in life, he was sensing emotions from those who walked in the afterlife. More protection was needed. More safety. Stronger powers to keep them at bay. Anything so he could be normal and have a life like everyone else.

Then one night he had a dream that was different from the others. The colors were more vibrant, making him feel he was awake instead of being fast asleep in his bed.

Alex found himself standing on a baseball diamond. In his hands he held a baseball bat. In the distance, on the pitcher's mound, he saw a figure whose face was obscured, throwing an orange ball at him. Instinctively, he batted it away. The pitcher continued throwing these bright orange balls at him and he continued batting them away. The intensity of the pitching increased until it was all Alex could do to keep up with batting away the balls. Although it was a dream, the constant batting began to take its toll both mentally and physically. He was growing exhausted. Yet the pitcher continued to volley balls at him.

Just as he felt he could no longer lift his arms, he suddenly heard a distinctive voice call out, "Stop!" Grateful to give his body a much-needed rest, Alex dropped the bat and stepped away. To his amazement, the pitcher continued to throw balls at the empty batter's mound until he became exhausted and stopped. When Alex awoke, he knew the dream had been significant, but he couldn't quite figure out exactly what it was trying to tell him.

A few months later, another opportunity to learn presented itself in a dream. Once again, a vibrant dream presented itself – deeper and fuller in its color than the first. This time, rather than being in the middle of the action taking place, he found himself observing from a distance. He thought it strange that he'd be watching from a place of observation, but instinctively knew something important was about to present itself.

He saw that he was sitting in a row of bleachers overlooking an orange football field. On the field were two teams. One was dressed in white, the other in black. Each was facing off, anxiously waiting for the game to begin. Suddenly, the football was kicked and the action began. Alex watched as they played, neither team advancing or gaining any significant amount of yardage. The longer he watched, the more it dawned on him that neither team was going to win. Nor was either team going to lose.

The teams went back and forth, back and forth. With fascination, Alex noticed the vibrancy of the orange field grow in brightness or turn dingy, as if the orange was mixed with mud. Each time the color changed, it was in response to how much energy the players themselves were putting into the need to win. To Alex, it became important not who won the game, but the overall feeling of the field itself. If the teams were neutral and not advancing, the field glowed a brighter orange. But when a battle ensued where each team tried to take the advantage and prove they were the better team, their energy muddied the orange and the color of the field turned a dirty brown.

When Alex awoke, he was both perplexed and intrigued by the strange dream. At the same time, he knew he was being taught something important in the dreamtime. Naturally he focused on the colors. What was the significance of the orange, the black, the white? What did they mean? Did colors have something to do with why he wasn't enjoying his own personal journey?

Alex was now in his teenage years. His need to fit in had become more acute. The peer pressure to fit in, to be the best, to compete, whether in sports or for girls, grew. He knew this energy was not the most truthful of energies, as teenagers, including himself, sought to push the boundaries, to discover who they were and where they fit in. Still, knowing this didn't help Alex with the heaviness of the emotions around him. Once more, he turned to his places of safety, his protection techniques to get him through each day. To his dismay, he found nothing seemed to be working anymore. It was as if the world he found so dear to him – the forest, the stones, the magical places, the areas of retreat – could not hide him from his teenage experiences. His anxiety increased. Even the thought of going to school each day brought him to a place of worry and fear. He did his best to shut down his feelings, but even as his own physical body was changing, the energy was also interfering with any sense of security. Surviving each day became the most important factor in his life.

As his friends and classmates planned for college, immersed themselves in relationships, planned for their futures, Alex found himself sinking deeper into despair as those things his friends found so significant held no interest for him. His constant thought was: How do I survive all this? Why is my world so different from everyone else's? What is wrong with me?

Even the vibrant dreams shut down. He turned to prayer, asking, begging that he be shown something, anything, that could help him maneuver his way through his life in a sane, healthy manner.

Then one night, a teacher presented itself.

He laid in bed, contemplating the feelings of the day, the experiences he'd had. The house was silent. Everyone, except Alex, was asleep. Staring at the ceiling, he thought he heard a swoosh, as if someone were outside his bedroom door. He cocked his head and listened. Just as he thought it was his imagination, he heard it again: a rustling as if dry leaves were piling up outside his door. He lifted his head and stared into the gloom of the darkened bedroom. Suddenly, to his horror, he watched a dark shadow materialize from the blackness and slowly approach him. His mouth grew dry; his heart hammered in his chest. The shadow approached his bed and hovered over him. Alex opened his mouth to scream, but nothing came out. His terror increased when he realized he couldn't move, couldn't escape. All he could do was lie on his back and stare up at the malevolent shadow that floated above him.

In his fear-addled brain, Alex realized that his life force was literally being drained out of him by this thing. He frantically tried to recall the protection modalities he'd learned. He used them all. Nothing happened. He tried praying, calling on every deity from every religion he'd read about. Still nothing happened. His body grew heavier, weaker. He felt he was dying.

He tried to reach for his crystals and stones, but his limbs were paralyzed. Abruptly, a little light broke through the terror in his mind. He remembered the vibrant dreams: the pitcher who stopped pitching balls at him once Alex stopped batting them. He remembered the football teams he'd observed that, when they stopped competing with each other, the field became more vibrant and the light grew. In the midst of the memories, he once again heard a strong voice yell out, "Stop!"

In that moment, he let go of his fear.

To his amazement, Alex watched as a swirl of vibrant orange began to emanate from all around him, illuminating his bedroom and illuminating the dark shadow floating over him. He watched as the color seemed to annoy and bother the shadow.

Alex quickly surrendered more to this orange field. He saw that the less he engaged his fears with the shadowy figure, the more pure and vibrant the orange became. The orange became so intense that the very room began to fill with white light. The stronger the white light became, the calmer Alex became.

His lack of fear interacted with the figure and it began to break apart until it finally disappeared.

His paralysis and lethargy gone, Alex sat up in bed and contemplated what had just happened. He didn't know where the white light had come from. From him? From somewhere outside him? Could he really be that strong? Despite all the questions, there was one thing Alex was very sure of: for the first time in his life, he felt in complete control. By surrendering, by not engaging, by not protecting, something had radically changed.

In Alex's need to protect himself and feel safe, he did whatever he could to bring himself some kind of a semblance of a normal life. This is a common occurrence as humans try their best to fit in, especially those who are empathic. There are those who turn to addiction, some remove themselves, and others spend money on all sorts of crystals, stones, sprays, all guaranteed to make them feel safe. Some empaths have the gift of bi-location, the ability to leave their physical bodies. If someone is not in their body, they don't need to feel.

Many empaths find themselves searching for answers in religion. Religious beliefs and customs have always been perceived as a way to find answers to our existence as souls encased in physical forms.

However, many religions, through no fault of their own, do not provide answers for the difficulties an empath faces in everyday life. They don't teach the mechanics of energy and how it works and why some people physically feel energy more than others.

In Alex's quest for answers, he would find nuggets of information from different historical texts on how to keep safe.

However, therein lay the problem.

His understanding of his empathy to this point was the need to feel safe. However, in his quest to feel safe, Alex was actually keeping himself separate from the world. The more he tried to protect himself from the outside world, the more he unwittingly attracted those energies to him that he was trying to protect himself from. He found himself living in a classic "Catch-22."

It may be hard for someone reading this book to accept the fact that there are helpers, watchers, and teachers on the Other Side who are always waiting for the opportunity, the right energetic opening, to present themselves to plant the seeds of truth. But they are there, waiting to help. You will know they are the right teachers for you by what you feel in your heart. If it feels right and fills your heart, go with it. If not, ask that your appropriate teachers be brought to you.

So it was with Alex in the dreamtime. In the dream state, the subconscious is more open. The mind is less prone to direct what is seen and experienced on a conscious level. The "logical" part of our brain shuts down, allowing the more emotional and intangibles that cannot be physically touched to come forward to be experienced. In the subconscious, the mind is more astute in its ability to project and perceive subtle energies.

People are not aware that as they delve into the thought process of protection, energy manifestation begins to grow. Protection declares: I am afraid. I am afraid, so I attract more of those things I am afraid of to me. That is how powerful the human mind is.

Many human prayers are born from the place of an empath's will. It comes from a place of their own needs, their own wants. Yet, in the needing and wanting to feel safe, they are also given valuable opportunities in which to learn. Here is where the teachers come in to provide those opportunities and lessons.

How will you as an empath learn to overcome fear if you are always protecting and running away from all you fear? As with Alex, that dark shadow turned out to be the very best thing to ever happen to him. Without that shadowy figure, Alex never would have realized that the only real protection that will always work is having no fear at all.

Fear cannot root itself in truth. As illustrated in the previous chapter, when Alex's mother brought him to the place of her fear regarding how the innocence of her child was being abused, it changed Alex's experience with the boys on the bus. That experience in turn changed Alex's own judgment about his perceived loss of his own power. He'd never really lost his own power. In his desire and need to fit in, he himself had given it away.

In his dealings with the physical heaviness in his own body, brought on by feeling everyone else's emotions, Alex put his energies outside himself. He placed blame on outside forces, saw himself as a victim or adversary. Just as he had the power to create walls and wield prayer in any manner to feel safe, he also had the power to create realities based on the untruth of his fears. He had not realized yet that the energetic experiences he was being allowed to partake in were teaching him a greater truth. The light was the key.

In his first dream, the baseball was orange.

For those familiar with the human chakra system, the second chakra, or sacral, is orange in color. The sacral chakra allows us to experience our lives through feelings and sensations. It is the center of emotion, pleasure, sensuality, intimacy, and connection with others. The challenge of this chakra is in not allowing ourselves to become disconnected from our bodies, our feelings, or our emotions in order to fit in and conform to what society feels we should conform to.

How many times in our own lives has someone thrown something at us – a thought, an emotion, a judgment – and we've reacted by hitting it back? How many of these games have continued for many years, almost taking on a life of their own, being fueled and fed from a place that we may not even remember? What started the situations? Are there times when we observe these games in others? Where we've watched friends or family, or complete strangers bicker, jockey for position, compete where one tries to get something on another, seeming to take away the other's very right to be – their very right to be present, their very right to feel safe in their own feelings and dealings with their inner and outer world? Have we learned from these situations? Have we found ourselves finding some kind of solace in the fact that it's not us or maybe looking from a place of our own judgment? What have we gotten from these things? From the moment? Is it possible that we received an energy?

In the first dream, as Alex heard the word "stop," he began to detach from the competition of the pitch of the orange ball that was projected at him. By detaching, he regained his strength. Is it possible that the message someone is pitching at us is their true desire for us to hit the ball back to them? Or maybe in their cleverness of making the greater pitch, as we swing and miss, there is some kind of revelry on their part that we missed, thus manifesting that energy into what we receive from them? In that moment, we allow ourselves to feel smaller while they grow because we've given our energy to them.

When Alex stopped batting the ball, there was nothing for the pitcher to gain anymore. There was no opportunity for the pitcher to revel that he was more able, more skillful in tricking Alex into missing. When Alex surrendered, he was no longer giving his energy to the pitcher. The pitcher had no choice but to stop pitching to an empty batter's mound.

As the second dream unfolded where Alex was the witness, once again the colors took center stage. Why was the field orange? Why were the players black and white? As the black and white players disengaged, the colors adjusted accordingly, rising in vibration and vibrancy, filling the field.

Lastly, in the dealings with the dark shadow, why was it that the more he engaged, the more Alex lost his power? The sense of powerlessness was what actually led Alex to the answer he'd been seeking for so long.

There is no shame in surrendering. And therein lies the key.

Everything in this world has its own need for energy. Each energy of this world is here for us to experience. Fear impedes this ability to experience. Rather than experience and learn and start to live in your own truth, you are instead living in an untruth, which is created by fear.

When Alex found himself in his safe place in nature or in those places of solitude where the energy was allowed to flow, without fear or worries, he was experiencing his highest truth. This place of highest truth is a place of energetic love, where no fear is perceived – where you know you'll be all right, no matter what.

As an empath, you are allowed to experience, in so many ways, the energies of all things in this world. Good, bad, white, black, life, death, have, have-not. Each is a label on how energy can be quantified or judged so that the experience can be understood from a logical mindset.

This, however, does not work with an empath.

As an empath, you feel energy with your physical body, your heart, your very soul. Each experience is an opportunity to realize your empathic power when you label the energy as good or bad. Remember, you have an amazing ability to manifest because of your sensitivity to energy. Therefore, when you label an energy as bad, you call more bad to you.

Just as you create walls, cast spells, pray, ask for assistance to bring into being all manner of energetic experiences, it is the same with what you fear. You create your own energetic reality from a place of thought and belief. However, the truth will find its way through those little cracks in your protective wall. How will you know? You'll know when you put up all manner of protection, yet your physical body is still experiencing the heaviness, the negative, the fear.

As Alex learned to create walls, he had to use his own energy as building material. The more protection he put up, the more of his own energy he had to use. Just as in the dream with the pitcher, he had to keep using his own energy to keep batting away the balls. The more he batted, the more exhausted he became.

When we lose ourselves in the need to win, the need to be right, the need to be in power, the need to be in control, none of these are rooted in energetic truth. Each of these are a label and are rooted in fear because they come from a place or a belief of lack.

The protection techniques eventually stop becoming effective because, as a physical being, your body is still taking on energy whether you like it or not. You can't stop it. Even if you isolate yourself in a dark bedroom, you're still taking on energy.

Pure energy from upstairs (or Source, or God, or whatever you believe in) comes into you every day. This is what connects us to the universe – to an energy or a being bigger than ourselves. There's nothing you can do about that – it just happens. This energy moves through you. Ideally, if you've healed and removed major blocks within you, the energy will flow through you and out your feet. It's a continuous motion twenty-four hours a day, seven days a week – the energy comes in through your crown from Source, moves through your feet into the earth. However, if there are blocks or fears within you, when the energy comes in, it will encounter the blocks and remain stuck. Over time, this stuck energy builds up. It has nowhere to go because it's not moving through you and out your feet. This stuck energy is what causes pains, illnesses, and an overall feeling of not being comfortable in your own skin. Therefore, shutting yourself away isn't going to stop you from feeling. You may not feel others' dysfunctions, but you'll feel your own.

We're sure many of you know people who love to instigate arguments. They pick and pick until someone explodes. The person exploding leaks their energy; the instigator gets that energy. The angered person exhausts themselves, while the instigator is refreshed. On a conscious level, they may not be aware of what they're doing, but look around you. Look at the television and see the reactions elicited by the nightly news. It's usually the emotions of fear and anger. There is a great deal of polarization going on right now. Whenever we react, who is getting that energy?

Unfortunately, we humans have learned to take energy from each other. The pure energy we're given everyday gets stuck behind the dam of our fears and blocks. It is also easily fed upon by others who have learned to get their energy from other people.

With each situation where Alex allowed himself to overreact, he leaked his own energy and actually called more unpleasant things and situations to him. He was, in essence, shouting out, "Yes, I'm afraid of all these things." By continually fearing and running away from these experiences, he was encountering more of what he was running away from. Once he stopped resisting and reacting and put the bat down, as he saw himself do in his dream, the energy that was coming at him had nowhere to go.

One more piece of the puzzle of what it meant to be an empath fell into place. Once he understood what he was doing with his energy and how he was allowing himself to be manipulated into reacting and leaking his energy, he was ready for the next building block in the foundation he was building.

Believe it or not, the next step in Alex's education of what being an empath is all about is one of the hardest steps for a human to take. It takes much courage to lift up the rock of your life and look at all those fears that eat away at you. Why are you afraid of being unloved? Of not being accepted? Of being ridiculed? Where does it stem from? Sometimes your fear may be a remnant from a past life. Perhaps you don't remember or know from where the fear stems. Maybe the fear is so traumatic you can't look at it again. What's important here is not living over again in detail the trauma that created a particular fear. What you need to do is feel the energy of the fear itself. As you feel that energy, you can begin to ground it out.

Why do we advocate peering into those dark places in your soul? Because healing your fears will be the best protection you will ever find. Trust us on this. We've spent years looking and healing all those fears we're writing about here. As we wrote about in our book *Ghost and Shamanic Tales of True Hauntings*, we have dealt with some of the darkest energies from the Other Side that you can imagine. But we came out unscathed. Because we've faced and healed our fears.

Think of your fears as a set of coat racks. Something comes at you that you fear, you react, and the fear attaches itself to those coat racks you carry within yourself. But once you heal the fears, you remove those coat racks. The next time an energy comes at you that you no longer fear, and more importantly, no longer fight against, there is nothing for it to attach itself to and it falls away.

The bottom line is that everything is energy. We muck up the works by labeling and attaching a story to our fears. "I'm frightened of love because so and so rejected me years ago," or "I can't deal with people, so I'm hiding away in my bedroom." Allowing yourself to feel your fear without attaching a story to it allows the energy to move quickly with you. Without the "coat rack," which is your fear, there is nothing for it to hold onto and it will flow through you.

It also helps to see what you're going through in the bigger picture. There's a reason these situations are happening to you. Everything you go through in life serves as a lesson. Unfortunately, we humans are pretty stubborn. Sometimes we need to be hit over the head over and over again until we figure things out. Knowing there's a method to the madness in your life makes it a little easier to deal with, especially when you realize that you're not the only one going through it. Comprehending the reasons – the fact that you're learning what it means to be an empath, how energy works, and making peace with the process – is a great beginning to getting through all the crazy stuff.

Why go through all of this angst? Because you are the example to others. Through your energy, you are that light to those who are still immersed in the "I have to be the best," "I have to compete," "I must succeed at all costs" mentality. As you get off the merry-go-round and no longer add to the miasma of energy around you, you stay in the energy of truth. You add more light to darkness. Darkness is simply an absence of light. As you heal your fears, you physically feel better, your vibration increases, your light increases. It can't help but affect those around you. It's that simple.

GROUNDING

Initially, as children and teenagers, we have to protect ourselves to feel safe. But as we grow and become stronger and have a higher understanding of how to bring in energy, instead of taking it from each other, we learn the best protection is no fear. With no fear, we begin to unlearn those dysfunctional habits we learned at a young age to keep ourselves safe. They don't serve us as adults because we're trying to grow into something stronger, so we release the need to be aloof, the need to disassociate ourselves from ourselves, to not overreact or hide in the shadows. It actually draws more to you to make you learn that lesson. It's getting to a place where you feel comfortable in your own skin no matter what. Remember, nothing can really harm you unless you allow it to harm you by your judgment of what the situation is – and how you react to that situation.

The following technique, called grounding, helps tremendously when you feel overwhelmed with emotions, whether yours or someone else's.

This is one of the basic steps to what being an empath is all about – the ability to move and change energy.

Grounding is a technique where you literally ground out any emotions, whether yours or someone else's, that adversely affect you and keep you from feeling your best.

Close your eyes and imagine a round, red ball about a foot beneath the soles of your feet. Focus your attention on this red ball. The more you focus on this ball, the more you should begin to feel your emotions slowly moving from your head, down through your chest and stomach, slowly cascading down your abdomen and legs and out the bottom of your feet into this ball. You may feel your feet tingling and you will begin to feel lighter the more you do this. Grounding really is that simple. The more you do this, the more you will train your body to automatically ground.

If you encounter someone whose emotional baggage bothers you, picture their energy rising from the top of their head, entering the top of your head and moving through you down into the little red ball beneath your feet. The important part here is not to "own" the energy you're processing. Do not attach a story to it. Do not judge it. Remember, you're simply a vessel moving the energy down into the earth. If you attach a story or a judgment, it has more of a chance to attach to you. Remember, your job as an empath is to change the energy. You do this by putting high vibrational energy into low vibrational energy.

After a few moments you will see either one of two things happen: (a) the person you've encountered will start to lighten up because you're moving their energy; or (b) they move away from you because they're not getting a reaction from you. No reaction means no leakage of your energy. They don't get it from you; they move away to get it from someone else.

3

Better to Keep Quiet

Everyone wants to fit in, including an empath. But as you try to understand your gift, you tell your stories to others who don't understand or they ridicule you. You learn very quickly to keep quiet. Why, when the truth of what you are seeking lies in tapping into the vibrational energy of love?

Any way you look at it, there's a universal truth about empaths: You're not like everyone else.

It only takes one experience to make that crystal clear. How do you tell your parents that you're seeing ghosts in your room? How do you tell your friends that someone is not what they appear to be? How do you tell others who don't feel as acutely as you do that the energy you're feeling at any given moment is lousy?

One of the hardest lessons for an empath to experience, especially when that person is a child, is how to navigate the outside world in order to feel "normal," or to operate under the radar so they don't call attention to themselves, or conversely, calling attention to themselves when the energy of that feels good. What happens when they leave the safety of their family and venture out to school for the first time?

Alex was excited about his new life as a student. Mingled with his excitement was a bit of trepidation. Would his school experiences be similar to those experiences when he'd been dragged out by his family to situations where he'd felt uncomfortable? Would he not fit in? By this time, family life itself was becoming difficult for him as his parents forced him into more and more unpleasant situations where he felt fearful and heavy with energy. School couldn't be any worse than that. Could it?

It was the first recess in kindergarten. Out on the playground, all the children who knew each other gathered into their own little exclusive groups.

As an unusually tall and new kid in the school, Alex stuck out. He went from group to group, hoping to start a conversation, hoping they would let him in. Because of his size, he wasn't afraid of physical confrontation in that way little boys have of testing each other out. He was, however, on guard with what he would say. Could he talk about his fantasy worlds where he felt safe? Could he discuss the connection he had with the trees and the animals and the stones?

It wasn't long before a boy approached him holding a football. The boy was shorter than Alex, with large brown eyes and dark hair. He looked up at Alex and smiled.

"Hey, I'm Billy," he greeted in such a friendly manner that a small piece of Alex's protective armor melted away.

"I'm Alex."

"Wanna play ball?"

"Sure."

To Alex's delight, they started tossing the football back and forth. After a few moments of this, Billy called out, "So what do you do for fun?"

Alex shrugged. "I spend time in the woods and play with my things," he answered.

"What kind of things?"

"Ah, you know, Army stuff."

"You mean like toy soldiers and tanks?"

Alex nodded.

"Why do you play with those?"

By this time, the two boys had been tossing the ball back and forth for fifteen minutes. Billy's energy felt good to Alex. The young boy was friendly and accepting and Alex felt a glimmer of hope that he'd found a new friend in school. Before he fully realized what he was saying, he blurted out, "They make me feel good. I play battle like I used to do."

"What do you mean 'like you used to do'?"

"I don't know. I just remember being in different wars and battles and ordering my soldiers to go here or there."

"Huh? That's weird." Billy turned towards a group of boys on the other side of the playground. "Hey guys, come over here and meet this weird kid."

The energy of feeling good, of being accepted, instantly evaporated. Now the energy became one of Alex trying to validate himself and prove to these boys that he wasn't weird. Those quiet moments when he'd played with his soldiers and relived his prior lives, those moments that had once given him comfort, were now being judged by others. He felt their judgment deeply. How could the things that made him feel safe and reassured now be so harshly judged by others?

For the rest of the day, Alex remained locked behind his wall of silence. He withdrew to that safe place inside himself where he wouldn't need to feel the judgmental or harsh energies of the boys and other students.

Days went by. The classwork became harder. Still, Alex found himself liking the school. He especially liked his music classes. A great deal of state-wide attention was given to the music program; it was one of the best in the state. It was here that Alex was introduced to music. He reveled in those moments when he found himself discussing beats and notes with other students who loved music as much as he did. He dove into the study of music, picking songs apart, intrigued by the complexity yet beauty that these little black dots on the sheet music could produce. He felt accepted because he knew this was something he was good at. He had a natural talent for it and it eased his loneliness.

One day, while out on the playground, he was sitting, as usual by himself, playing quietly with his marbles. It had been weeks since his encounter with Billy and his friends and although he remained wary, he'd managed to push their behavior out of his mind.

To his dismay, he found a presence at his elbow. Looking up, he saw it was Billy and his ever-present gang of boys.

"Hey weird kid," they greeted. "What are you doing?"

At first Alex refused to answer. Would they ridicule him again? Did he really want to go through that? Yet not to answer would bring more scorn upon him. So he casually shrugged his shoulders. "Just playing with my marbles. See?"

He hit a number of marbles with another.

"That's stupid. You're just hitting dumb marbles."

Alex grew angry. "No, I'm not!" he exclaimed. "I'm making a song like the teacher said. Every time I hit the marble, I make a sound. A couple of sounds make a rhythm."

To his chagrin, the boys didn't understand what he was doing. They couldn't feel the joy he was getting by creating notes and cadences with the marbles. Instead, they laughed and called him weird again.

As they walked away, Alex felt his energy plummet. Once again something that was bringing him happiness was creating a judgment that turned his happiness into sadness and anger. Once again he was forced to see that he just didn't fit in.

He started to question his experiences. Was it better to speak or better to stay quiet? Why was it that those things that made him feel good were actually a detriment to him developing friendships with his classmates? What was it about him that made him stand out and be different and not allow him to blend and fit in? Why couldn't he share those things that made his soul sing with delight and wonder?

As Alex disengaged from those around him, he put up a wall of protection around himself. It kept him isolated. He thought it made him feel safe. But what the wall was actually doing was making it more difficult for him to make friends and interact with the living.

This is when the interaction with the Other Side began.

As a young child, Alex did not yet know that you could not hide from energy because energy does not just come from the living. It also comes from those that dwell in the in-between place – that area that lies between the world of the material and the world of spirit.

He began to see faces peering at him while he lay in bed at night. He began to hear whispers in his ear, yet when he turned to see who it was, there was no one there. People would appear to him while he played out in his backyard, becoming those playmates he yearned for. What others considered a fantasy world became Alex's reality.

He became obsessed with war, with the study of history. These people from the in-between place told him things that, when shared with his parents, left them worried and afraid. How could such a young child know about events that happened centuries before he was born? How could a six year old know about religious prophecies that spoke of the end of times?

When Alex's obsession turned to flying saucers and the existence of extraterrestrials, they grew frantic. Their boy was not normal. There had to be something wrong with him. What was so real to Alex in those moments when he was alone with his thoughts and feelings were causing his parents endless nights of worry. In an effort to get a handle on this, they forbade Alex to speak of such things.

In the face of their concern, he began to question this obsession he had. Why did he need to know such things? Why did the knowledge of prophecy or of wars fought long ago bring him such a sense of familiarity, as if they were an integral part of his very being?

Despite their admonishment not to talk about such things, as he grew older, Alex began to venture out beyond his wall of silence and tentatively bring up these forbidden subjects. The world was changing and the subject of past lives, ghosts, and prophecy was becoming more prevalent. If his questions were perceived with openness, he could pursue the subject because their openness was an energetic permission for him to be himself – to share his curiosity with others. At the same time, this energetic permission also made him more empathic.

It was becoming easier to physically feel the true intentions of those he spoke with about his inner life. He felt their awkwardness at his words, their puzzlement of who this kid was who thought such deep thoughts. He also perceived, to his surprise, their awkwardness with themselves. While Alex appeared so self-assured with his own knowledge and curiosity, they still struggled to discover who they were and where they fit into the world at large. For the first time, Alex saw the separateness, yet the sameness in everyone. Despite humanity's obsessive need to erect barriers, whether by the color of skin, sexuality, or religious beliefs and customs, he saw that humans were all alike. They all struggled with the same issues. He thought of the famous Shakespearean quote, spoken by a Jew to a Gentile, that summed up the oneness of us all: "If you prick us, do we not bleed? If you tickle us, do we not laugh? If you poison us, do we not die?"

Throughout his experiences, Alex grew to understand how humans deal with each other. Whether as adults or children, those who laughed and ridiculed him did so to make themselves feel better about themselves, empowering themselves by thinking: "He's crazy, thank God we're not."

Humans judge one another, find flaws in others, so they can hold power over one another. They keep a running tab of faults and use them, at a moment's notice, to take or trick someone into capitulating their motives or needs. They come forth with smiles and hands open, only to rip into the person once that person's back is turned. They speak badly of others as if they are in a vacuum, not knowing or caring that their hurtful words always find their way back to the person they are denigrating.

These realizations gave Alex valuable insight into his fellow humans. It also, unfortunately, affected him deeply on a physical and energetic level. His sensitivity to all this heavy emotional angst took its toll. When he was a teenager, his parents took him to a counselor.

By this time in his life, Alex had concluded it was better to keep the dreams, visions, visitations, and knowings to himself and say nothing. He couldn't bear the judgments, the ridicule, the censored looks of adults and friends. So he found himself in the counselor's office, staring at him, saying nothing.

Yet although Alex stayed silent, his senses were still alert. He noticed how the room in which they sat felt devoid of any feeling. It was as sterile as a hospital operating room. Unlike the forest and the privacy of his room where he felt happy and safe, this office was a place of nothingness.

It unnerved him.

A silent battle of wills took place. The counselor sat and stared at Alex. Alex sat and stared at the counselor. Each side waited for something to be said. Alex's senses told him the counselor was waiting for him to speak – to divulge a secret, to discuss his inner life. Yet, as with most empaths, Alex had perfected the state of being silent. He knew if he spoke the truth, something would change and probably not for the better. After all, this man was an adult. He held the power. The session continued. The silence continued. After the allotted hour, the session ended and Alex left.

Naturally his parents wanted to know how his session had gone. Alex shrugged and answered noncommittally. This ensured another visit to the counselor.

This time around, however, Alex learned a valuable lesson. He hated sitting in that sterile room, being stared at by this formidable man. He wanted nothing more than to escape. But how? What could he do to get the hell out of this situation and back to his place of safety?

Alex leaned forward in his chair and noticed the counselor do the same. He felt the counselor's energy shift into an expectant "Ah, let's see what this boy is going to say" attitude.

"I'm going to be okay, you know," Alex spoke slowly. "I just need to pick some new friends and make an effort to fit in a little more. I'm going to get a job and make some money. Become more responsible."

There was an instant change in the air. A brief smile flickered across the counselor's face. To Alex's amazement, the room no longer felt sterile and dead. His words had somehow made the counselor feel special because he had cured Alex. His smile was an acknowledgment that Alex's plan was a good one, a plan he wholeheartedly approved of.

The energy in the room now felt good to Alex. He felt the counselor's approval. His love for this misfit boy. A shift now occurred within Alex. At that moment, he learned how to please people and have them approve and love him by telling them exactly what they wanted to hear.

That now became his mantra. Tell folks what they want to hear and they'll like me. They'll include me in things. They'll make me a part of their group, their lives. I'll have friends and I won't stick out anymore.

What Alex didn't realize was that his people-pleasing was just another lesson on his path to understanding his gift of empathy.

Those of us who grew up empathic learned at an early age what it feels like when you say something that doesn't jibe with another's thought process. There's an immediate dualistic reaction – it's black or white, good or evil. No gray areas. The energy feels horrible and you immediately clam up because who wants to keep feeling that disapproving energy?

Parents who don't understand empathy and what their child is going through will go the counseling route as Alex's parents did. Children who feel too much will be given medication to deaden their reactions. They go from feeling everything to feeling nothing. Yet what is truly being accomplished? We're here to experience, to involve ourselves, to feel in order to understand and learn who we are and where we fit into the scheme of things. Taking away that ability to feel and to experience is condemning the child to miss out on so much. To cry at the exquisite beauty of a sunset. To change the energy of those around them by changing their own energy. To start changing the world by changing themselves.

There is also an awakening that goes along with being an empath. As we've stated here (and will continue to state), everything has an energy to it. Including the dead.

Many empathic children speak about seeing ghosts in their rooms, or of knowing when something is going to happen before it happens. Because empaths are so sensitive to energy, they can breach the veil between the worlds of the living and the dead and have interaction with those who have passed.

We've discovered in our work with the Other Side that ghosts are those people who are still burdened with the heavy energies of anger, guilt, unfinished business, etc., who were never healed in life. Yet they no longer have a physical body to release those emotions. Because of an empath's abilities to sense those emotions, they can "ground them out" for the dead. This is one of the things they are very good at doing.

We're sure many of you reading this book have had the experience of sitting on your couch, watching television, feeling pretty good, when all of a sudden, for no reason whatsoever, you feel sad. Or angry. Or any other type of emotion you weren't feeling five minutes before. What's happened is that a spirit who was still earthbound entered your energy field. As an empathic person, you were picking up and feeling those emotions they could no longer release on their own. Rather than immediately going into fear (and feeding the spirit your fear), you can instead assist them by quietly grounding out their energy. Remember, energy is energy, no matter who or what it's coming from. If you can ground out your own energy or that of your living friends, you can ground out the energy of the dead as well.

A note here to those empaths who do feel or deal, whether they want to or not, with the Other Side: When it comes to the paranormal, not everything you feel that makes you uncomfortable is evil, despite what you may hear or see on television. Ninety-nine percent of the time it's the dysfunction of a person who has never healed their issues in life and who are condemned to carry them in death until they are assisted in releasing their traumas. Drama in life equals drama in death. Whatever you were in life – be it compassionate, nasty, fearful, or a complete jerk – you're going to be that way in death, until you are assisted in releasing those heavier emotions and can leave the earthly plane.

If you don't understand the whys and wherefores of what is going on, you will become the type of empath who tries to control any given situation so you don't have to feel anything that doesn't feel good. You will throw up "shields" of protection, not realizing that by doing so, you may be preventing yourself from learning a very important lesson that will help you on the next step of your journey. Or you may be denying yourself of receiving a message from the Other Side that will assist you in some way.

We're often asked why we don't "shut off" our empathic and psychic abilities. We always remain open and are amused that people are amazed by that. Our thinking is this: What if a message is trying to come through that a meteorite is about to hit the area and we don't hear the warning to move to the left because we're shut off? Yes, that may be a bit extreme, but you get the idea. You never know what needs to get through, and by controlling this, you miss out on messages or lessons that are important to your growth as an empath.

If you don't allow yourself the opportunity to learn about energy, you also run the risk of denying the truth of who you are by becoming a people-pleaser who allows yourself to be molded into whatever your friends or partner needs. You live your life as a reflection of another's perception, never fully allowing your own spirit to emerge.

All of this condemns you from moving forward energetically. You don't allow yourself to experience the energy at any given moment and learn from it. Unlike the dead, you still have a choice to stop the merry-go-round. You can learn what you need to learn and move on.

Teenagers in particular are extremely sensitive anyway. Not only are they dealing with hormonal changes, but as they enter adulthood, they are discovering their own boundaries and beginning their journey to understand who they are. We're finding that young people and children are much more sensitive to the energies that surround us. As each prior generation fails to clean up the energetic morass around them and actually end up adding more to the mess, the following generations are born into this growing mishmash. Without a basic understanding, these young people pull back or shut themselves off. They become withdrawn or surly because no one understands what they're going through.

Yet shutting themselves off from the outside world only works for a little while. Regardless of where they are, they will feel things. It's simply the nature of the beast. The trick is not to think of themselves as freaks.

Millions of people are having the same experiences. Millions are awakening and seeing the Other Side. Millions are feeling the quagmire of turbulent emotions out there. It's just that this particular subject hasn't been spoken of very much because it's not looked at as a viable option. Who talks about grounding? Who talks about facing your fears? Who talks about the empath's job and responsibility to move and bring a sense of calmness to the chaotic energy that exists in the world today?

However, before you get to the point of accepting and understanding your responsibilities to yourself and to the world at large, you have two choices. You can shut yourself away, or learn not to say anything. Let's face it, everyone wants to fit in, regardless of age. Everyone wants to feel a part of something or someone else. Children in dysfunctional families try to make the situation better by being peacemakers. When this doesn't work, the withdrawal process begins, whether it's a physical withdrawal or a withdrawal fueled by alcohol and drugs.

There is one thing to keep in mind. Whenever you, as an empath, deny who you are, or you put out fear-based energy, you're adding more to what is already out there.

It's difficult when you're young to stand up and say: "Yes, I'm feeling this stuff." It's been our experience that eventually you will find like-minded people who can assist you along the way and help you understand why you feel what you feel. That's why we decided to write this book. We went through our early lives without someone to talk to about what we were feeling and experiencing. We had no one to turn to who understood us. We went through everything you'll find in this book alone. It doesn't need to be that way anymore.

The world is awakening to the concept of energy. We know things have to change at some point as we fall deeper and deeper into a pit of fear and polarity. But how do we change? What steps do we take to pull ourselves and those around us out of the seemingly never-ending cycle of fear and anger and withdrawal?

- Know that you're not alone.
- Know it's all right to feel all the things you feel.
- Practice the grounding.
- Try to look at the bigger picture.
- Start the baby steps by looking at your fears and confronting them and making peace with them.
- Know that what you're experiencing is just one more brick in the foundation of what you're building.

THE ENERGY OF TRUTH

Initially, the quietness is a way not to draw energetic attention. The lesson, however, is that the energetic attention you're trying so hard not to draw to yourself is another truth of who you are. Everything that is said, or is thought, or is put into motion, has an energy to it. Even being quiet and withdrawn is creating an energy. The lesson to learn from this is that every human being has an energetic voice. Words don't always reflect the energy of what you're feeling or what you've experienced. As an empath, you can sense in the moment what another needs by how their energy is being presented to you – which goes beyond words. So, what do you do with that? Do you put forth your own energy in response in a manner that gives the person what they want, regardless of what you want? Is this the right way? Or is this another lesson?

You take on so much energy whether you mean to or not. That's what being an empath is all about. However, as an empath, you have the ability to use your energy to put out, without words, who you are. You don't need to get reactions or push away reactions. Just being the energy speaks louder than words. It is the energy of truth. Of the person you are without hiding in the shadows. As you put out the energy of truth, others who come into your energy field can't help but be affected by it.

There's a saying in the New Age community: Just be. What that means is being who you are, without a façade, without a mask. Without the trappings of who you think people want you to be. It's having the courage to energetically say, "I am an empath. I see things, I feel things. I am what I am." It's being comfortable in your own skin and accepting the gifts you have with humility. Like energy attracts like energy.

So imagine for a moment what would happen if you began to radiate with the energy of truth. That energy will give someone else the courage to find and become who they are. You will attract like-minded people to you. It's how energy works.

And it will attract the next set of lessons for you to experience and learn from...

4

Why do I Get All the Bad Stuff?

Much of what is taught in the New Age Community does not address the deep healing necessary to face anything and everything that comes at you. When the energy turns bad, it all falls apart. Why? How does energy work and can you be strong when the energy does turn bad?

One of the realities of an empath's life is that we know how wonderful energy can feel because we've felt it. We experience so deeply the breathtaking, the sublime. At the same time, we also experience the stuff that isn't so wonderful: the heavy emotions that make us feel as though we're walking through sludge. The catch-22 of all this is that we strive desperately to get back to "wonderful."

As stated earlier, empaths come to this earth with a job to do. But as with every job, there's a learning curve. And it seems that those who are empathic have many energetic difficulties coming to them, starting in childhood. They're oftentimes born into dysfunctional families, or find themselves unable to fit in with schoolmates, or others. Events that seem so simple for others take on monumental proportions for the empath. Many times they suffer from nightmares, panic attacks, or anxiety. Those who are especially sensitive suffer from ghostly visitations, or seeing and experiencing things from the Other Side that the average person doesn't know about or understand. They also have visions of past or future events, leaving them often struggling with what reality truly is and isn't.

As with most empaths, Alex experienced all of this. Coming into his teenage years, he wondered why he wasn't having the same experiences as others around him. How was it that others had no problems forging friendships? Why was it that others could so easily align with sports, or extra-curricular activities while he found such things difficult to do? He just couldn't seem to easily embrace those undertakings that his friends and families found so simple. He desperately wanted normalcy. All the heaviness of his experiences were cocooning him and separating him from the world. He knew it was happening. But he didn't know how to change it.

He began to contemplate his existence. "Why?" became his mantra. "How?" became his quest. Fitting in at any cost, or finding a way to fit in, became his obsession. As an empath who was sensitive to emotional spaces in this world, the logical place for him to call his own was music. Like many teenagers, he developed separate musical tastes from the adults in his life.

At the time, heavy metal was what drew him into the world of music and musicians. He loved the bands with the screaming guitars, jungle-rhythm drumbeats, wild hair flying about as the musicians frenetically drove the music on and on. At this stage in Alex's life, he'd already gotten himself a guitar, and spent hours plucking out chords in the privacy of his room, accompanied by his favorite tunes. It was in that privacy, playing, albeit haltingly, where he found comfort.

One day, he was invited by a group of schoolmates to attend a heavy metal concert. At first he was hesitant. He grew anxious at the thought of being in the middle of a huge crowd of people, knowing how he reacted to all that crazy, swirling energy. Yet, he loved this band's music. He didn't want to miss out on such an exciting experience. So he gathered his courage and accepted.

Arriving at the concert hall a few days later, the energy and power in the room was so formidable, he was mesmerized. The hollering, the foot stomping, the whistles drew him in. Then the lights lowered. The screaming intensified. The foot stomping grew louder. Through the murky darkness he could just make out the band scurrying across the stage to their instruments. He held his breath.

Suddenly, an explosion of light and fog tore open the darkness and there the band stood, ripping into the audience with a guitar riff that almost brought the house down. With their long hair and black skin, tight clothes, their vocals echoing throughout the hall, they were in complete control of the audience. Alex's jaw dropped. He'd never felt energy like that before. Looking about him, he could physically feel the adoration, the love, the lust of the audience moving up towards the stage. Those four men held the power of the audience in their hands. They knew it. They reveled in it. They owned it. In that moment Alex knew he had to have this. No matter what he had to do to achieve it, he too was going to experience that power, that energy one day.

Arriving home after the concert, he threw himself obsessively into playing his guitar. Over and over he practiced until his fingers bled. But he kept at it. It wasn't long before his skill grew. It also wasn't too long before his guitar playing began to attract like-minded friends into his orbit. They quickly formed a band and spent every waking hour practicing, learning new songs, trying new chords. The camaraderie, the similar obsession, the shared love of the music felt so good to Alex. His energy was being used for something other than hiding and keeping the negativity of others at bay. The band expanded as they added a drummer and a singer. The music grew to having a life of its own: its own energy.

It was wonderful.

For the first time in his life, Alex felt that he belonged to something bigger than himself. He'd finally found a niche where he fit right in.

There at last came a time when the band needed to get out and play in front of people. A few friends who had heard them practice decided to have a party and they were invited to play.

That first engagement led to more engagements. People like to align to something successful, and Alex's band was growing in success and popularity. Suddenly, others wanted to be his friend. Alex's proficiency with the guitar and the attention it was garnering gave him a personality. His self-esteem grew in leaps and bounds. Rather than being an object to shun, he now became an object of adoration. It was heady stuff for a young man. But starved for such attention for so long, he reveled in it.

High school ended and now he was in college. The band was bigger than ever. However, along the way, something was happening that Alex didn't quite grasp at first. He didn't realize that he was losing himself. Rather than being just Alex, an offbeat guy who looked at the world a little differently, he was now being identified as a "Musician." All those parts of Alex that had been molded into an understanding and learning of his energetic world now turned outward. Rather than being validated by his own energy and the energy from Source, all his validation was coming from the label that he was now a Musician.

As it is with most empaths, this external validation will eventually crash and burn because it isn't aligned with truth. Yet, as with every experience, it served its purpose as a valuable lesson to add to Alex's growing tool box of lessons.

In the meantime, Alex's band was booked months in advance. He'd begun to write their own material, opening doors for them to record. There were days Alex would walk down the street and be recognized by adoring fans. He found himself attracted to this worship. This must have been what the Beatles felt, or Elvis, or any of the famous bands he admired. He loved the attention and acceptance he'd never had as a child. It became almost like an addiction to him. All that adulation seemed to fill the holes he carried inside. It never lasted. But there was always the next gig where he'd fill up again with an energy that he didn't realize was illusory, since he had to keep refilling himself with it over and over again.

For the time being, however, it was exhilarating.

The band continued to grow in reputation and popularity. They were now traveling throughout New England and playing in more bars and clubs. Each night, Alex found himself immersed in all this divergent energy. Each night, he allowed himself to react to all that energy. And each morning, he stumbled around in exhaustion. It was more than physical exhaustion. It was an exhaustion of the soul. He was getting what he thought he'd wanted. He was popular. People loved him. He had more women chasing him than he knew what to do with.

Yet somehow it wasn't enough.

Instead of feeling filled up, he felt drained. Still, he continued his schedule, playing into the wee hours of the night and spending the next day barely functional. It was more than the late hours that was leaving him so tired. He just couldn't figure out what it was.

Analyzing it, he realized it had something to do with the fact that all those people wanted Alex to be something for them. Because he'd been labeled a Musician, there were standards they were holding him up to. He was expected to wear certain clothing, keep his hair a certain length, hold himself a certain way on stage, play his songs a certain way.

He strived to become what people wanted him to be. He now became obsessed with keeping his band on top. He pushed himself to become a better musician, write better songs, perform more outrageously on stage to keep the fans happy. He'd finally found something that made him feel wanted in this world. But it was starting to corrode. The energies that had once filled him were now slowing down, making him feel heavy again.

Eventually, the crash came. He wasn't feeling the same way on stage. Rather than take pleasure in the audience, he began to turn on them. Now, there was never enough of a crowd, never enough adoration. The music wasn't perfect enough. His fellow musicians weren't as serious about their careers as he was. Damn it, they didn't care as much as he did.

As the negativity built up inside of Alex, he turned to alcohol in an effort to dull the sensations. Yet there came a point where even the booze wasn't working. As it is with empaths, external things that are used to keep them in an internal state of calm don't last.

Having tried everything and seeing it wasn't working, Alex realized he had to go back to his old way of thinking – back to basics. He had to step back from his life and witness what was going on.

Why wasn't any of this working any longer? Why, whenever he stepped on stage, was the energy he felt heavy and uncomfortable? The people still liked him. They still clamored for his songs. They still wanted to be part of his experience.

At their next engagement, he stood on stage, scanning the audience and allowed the oppressive energy to envelope him. One part of his brain focused on his playing, the other logically dissected the energy he was feeling. Halfway through the first set, the answer came to him.

Looking out over the crowd, he realized many of them were there not just for the band or their music. They were there with their own agendas. They gathered together with others to forget about their own fears, their own neediness. They were there to pick up members of the opposite sex to lose themselves in the pleasures of the flesh, at least for one night. Their energies weren't matching up with their words or actions.

A few nights later, in between sets, Alex sat alone at the bar. By this time, he wasn't drinking because the drinking made him feel worse energetically. People came up to him, wanting to be his friend, wanting something from him, but he shooed them away. On that night, he just wanted to be left alone.

It took him a little while to realize someone was sitting on the bar stool next to him. He sighed. Crap, why couldn't people just leave him alone? Deciding the only place he could get some privacy was backstage, he started to get up to leave. However, just as he turned, he caught a glimpse of the person on the bar stool. She was a beautiful blonde woman with large green eyes and a warm smile. He hesitated.

"You're not having much fun up on stage tonight, are you?" she asked softly.

Alex sat back down. "Why do you say that?" he asked.

She shrugged. "It's pretty obvious."

Alex knew he should just get up and leave. He wasn't up to talking to anyone at that moment. But there was something about her – something more than just her beauty – that kept him seated. He matched her shrug with one of his own.

"Can't seem to get into the groove tonight," he found himself admitting. "We're playing okay, but I'm not feeling it. And if I'm not feeling it, it doesn't mean anything to me."

"I think I know what's going on." She spread her long slender fingers over the bar and turned to face him. "You're feeling everybody way too much. You're getting so much energy thrown at you while you're up on the stage, you're on overload. Instead of moving the energy out of you, it's all sticking to you like glue. And you're reacting to it. I bet every time you and your band play, you're exhausted the next day."

His eyes widened in surprise. "Yes, I am."

"I'll also bet you've been that way your whole life."

Alex was stunned. So much so, he didn't know what to say.

"Here's a little trick I learned that I'm sure will help you. You're a smart guy. See if you can picture a red ball beneath your feet."

Alex hesitated. Was this some kind of joke? Was this girl for real? His first instinct was to get up and walk away. But he didn't. Looking at her, he sensed her sincerity. Aw hell, he had nothing to lose. "I can do that," he responded.

Closing his eyes, Alex pictured a round red ball beneath his feet. Instantly, his toes began to tingle. He felt his weariness and the negativity he'd been struggling with slowly ooze down through his legs and out his feet. Now he felt energized. A memory danced before his closed lids. He'd done this before, years ago in his backyard, when he'd picked up a stone and felt the energy flow out of him. In the maddening course his life had taken, he'd completely forgotten about it.

"Feeling better?" she asked.

"Very. What's this called?"

"Grounding."

"Where did you learn to do this?"

"I'm an energy worker."

He frowned. "What's that?"

She smiled as she slid off the bar stool. "It's someone like you who thankfully figured it out. Pay attention, Alex. It will all start to make sense to you. Don't judge the energy you soak up. Don't label it. Just allow it to be. If you keep grounding, you'll be fine."

He watched as she disappeared into the crowd. He never saw her again after that night, but her words stayed with him, long after the memory of her face faded away.

That night, during their second set, he tried her technique. He felt the energy coming up at him from the audience. He felt the lust, the manipulation, the neediness, the sadness, the aggression. He felt all those emotions drape themselves over him. He felt it start to weigh him down. However, he remembered what the girl had told him. He abruptly stopped judging the energy, ceased putting a label to it. When he pictured the red ball, he was astonished to feel the energy move out of him quickly. Within a few moments, the oppressive energy was gone. It was easier being on stage now and the next day he found to his delight that he wasn't exhausted. A light bulb went off in his head.

I can be in the middle of a lot of crap and be okay.

He spent that day analyzing and dissecting what he was doing when he grounded. He realized that somehow, when he grounded out the energy, he was actually changing it. Instead of allowing these energies to stick to him and gather strength because of his own reaction and labeling of it, he'd actually been able to lighten up the energy and himself by not reacting to it. By not giving it a story to cling to.

He thought back to the day he'd stood in his backyard and held the stone. He remembered that the lightness he'd experienced hadn't lasted. Now he understood why. Each time he'd rid himself of the heavy energies, he'd judged and attached a story to subsequent energies, which made them cling that much stronger to him. However, if he didn't judge, if he didn't attach a story, the energy flowed through him quicker.

He had more "a-ha" moments. As a youngster he'd created a fantasy world because he couldn't deal with the trauma of a difficult family, or of feeling different from everyone else. He'd spent so much time fighting what he was feeling that he'd end up exhausted, yet it hadn't stopped him from feeling what was around him. The more he fought it, the more that became his energy. It became his vulnerability. It took him a moment to realize what a valuable lesson he'd been presented with, not only at this club, but in all the other bars and clubs he'd been playing.

Instead of reacting to the energy around him, all he needed to do was witness it, acknowledge it, and ground it. By not reacting and taking it on, he wasn't adding to the problem.

Buoyed by this revelation, he decided to take it one step further. At the next gig they played, he filled himself with the energy of unconditional love. Not a physical love, but a love borne of non-judgment. Of accepting each person in that club for who they were, no matter how they were dressed or how they were acting. He saw each person as being in the same boat he was in – trying to make it through each day whichever way they could. He then radiated that energy he was feeling out to the first few rows surrounding the stage. To his surprise, he saw and felt the heaviness dissipate from those nearest to him. He then expanded his energy to the entire room. Not all of the heavier energies completely disappeared, but the room did grow lighter.

By the time the evening ended, Alex was amazed at how different he felt. Rather than the usual exhaustion, he was energized. The more he thought about it, the more he understood what he'd done. Just as in other evenings, he'd taken on the energy of the room. However, unlike other evenings, he hadn't reacted to it. Instead, he'd moved out the lower vibrational energy by grounding it, then replaced it with the higher vibrational energy of non-judgmental love.

It was the beginning of his understanding on how energy worked. He didn't need to keep doing the protection stuff, nor shut himself down, nor pretend that negativity didn't exist. He just needed to be open to the experience. Because, as he found out the hard way, you can't hide from this stuff forever.

The more he hid, the more these experiences sought him out. Rather than plug into the situation, he ground out the energy and gained more control over his own energy. He realized that the more he hid, the less he got to experience that part of himself that could overcome the difficult situations. He didn't have to be the energy he was feeling. He didn't have to own it. He could move it out of himself and remain balanced.

The more he thought about it, the more he came to the conclusion that all he'd experienced up to that point had happened in order to teach him what an empath truly was – a person who could move energy. He began to understand the matrix of the physical body – how energy gets stuck to us, how the feelings of others get stuck to us. If he hadn't gone through the bad stuff, if he hadn't tried every protection method under the sun (and see that ultimately it didn't work), if he hadn't gone through keeping quiet of all he had experienced, he would never have been open to learning about moving energy. It simply would never have occurred to him. He laughed when he realized there really was a method to the madness.

Now, the next phase of his lesson began.

One day, while heading to work, he had a phantom anger come over him. As the energy enveloped him, he didn't react. He witnessed and ground. When he was done, he thought about what he'd just felt. What was that anger all about? A few days later, he woke up sad – almost to the point of tears. Once again, he allowed himself to simply witness it and noticed how quickly the energy moved through him.

This began to occur with more frequency. He'd suddenly experience an emotion he hadn't been feeling a moment before, yet through witnessing and grounding, he was able to move it through him quickly and retain his good humor. Curious, he tried to figure out what he was doing. It wasn't long before he discovered that as an empath, he could not only change the energy of the living, but of the dead as well.

With more spirits wandering the earth, stuck in the in-between place because they're still burdened with heavy human emotion, Alex found he could assist them by grounding out their emotions, since they no longer had a physical body to do that for themselves.

Through all of these incidents, Alex concluded that his life had meaning. The heavy, angry, sad, overwhelming moments were preparing him for something. No longer was his empathy a curse. He was being trained or allowed to experience so he could be of assistance to some kind of energetic change. In the moments when he accepted who he was and what he was feeling, it moved quicker through him. When he was in want, need, fear, or being another way with the energy, it got stuck longer.

As it got stuck, it attracted more spirits to him.

Each of the spirits that came to him were having the same energetic experience as Alex. One by one, those in the other realm that were stuck found their way to Alex. One by one, he experienced with them their living traumas of energy that kept them wandering. Some were angry, some were sad because they had to leave someone behind. Some felt guilt or some were worried that they hadn't finished what they'd come here for. As Alex allowed each spirit into his personal space and ground out their emotions, they lightened up as their emotional burdens were moved through him. He got stronger in this ability. Soon the living began to come to him, divulging their secrets, confiding in him, needing their own validations about what they were doing, where they were going and why.

As Alex sat with them, not judging, not labeling, but simply listening, their intentions and energy flowed through him. He found he no longer feared the heavy energies that had once overwhelmed him. He didn't feel uncomfortable anymore in crowds. He no longer hid from life. He'd made peace with the process – the gift of becoming an empath.

Spiritual Boot Camp

The bad stuff is a learning process. We call it spiritual boot camp. Just as a man or woman learns to be a soldier in military boot camp, you learn what it means to be an empath in spiritual boot camp. The end result is to be a light.

As an empath, you will begin to learn from your experiences. With each lesson learned, your own energy will begin to change. It will grow lighter. More accepting. Your energy in turn has the ability to change those around you. You are the stone that falls into the water and creates a ripple effect that will touch those you come in contact with.

As you learn to stop bargaining yourself away and stand in the truth of who you are, that energy allows others to do the same. It also allows you to deal with any kind of energy or event that comes at you. Remember, no matter what is happening, it's all energy. Once you grasp that, you find you don't need extraneous things to make you feel good or protected. You don't need crystals or sprays or calling in angels for protection. The power of protection, the ability to feel good, the freedom you feel when you've healed your demons all lie within you. You are better equipped to deal with the bad stuff when it happens.

If you perceive things as anger, then anger is what it becomes. If you look upon an experience as negative, then you have used your own energy to label it and feed it as so. It's not that we should see all things as fluffy, but to see all things as an experience to allow it to flow, to allow it to be what it is – the simple energy of experience. By not anchoring to labels or the need to change it to your paradigm of what you believe it should be, the energy finds its way back to Source.

What is the will of the energy of Source? To make a choice. It's that simple. It all comes down to making a choice out of a place of love or out of a place of fear.

Every choice you will ever make comes from these two places – love or fear. That is the duality of this world. It either fills you up or drains you out. This is the pattern of love and fear. It doesn't end until you realize love is all things, even fear, depending on how far you've evolved in your spiritual path. For example, an owl flies in total darkness, yet he sees light. A child throws a tantrum to get love, but first he has to fear that he won't have enough love. A person chooses to fill their life with material things because they fear lack.

An empath's experiences from a point of growth in one's ability to know true non-conditional love is what pushes us all forward to learn. As an empath, you will know when someone chooses from a place of fear. How? Because there's an absence of high vibrational love connected to the energy you're feeling from that person. When you choose the path of high vibrational love, the energy around you and within you increases. You have an "a-ha" moment – an instant where your lesson has been learned and the knowledge of what you've learned flows into you.

We each have been given choices. We cannot know the higher essences of love if we haven't come from the lower, physical aspects of love – of things, of ownership, of needing validation from another, each in its moment serving a purpose. These lower physical aspects of love don't last because they're not rooted in truth. You feel this because, as an empath, you're not feeling the peace and serenity that high vibrational love gives you. You quickly realize how people get stuck in their lives because they keep choosing fear; the fear of not having enough possessions, enough money, enough adulation, enough power. You feel this as heaviness. When you begin to accept each moment for what it is and walk your journey with openness, excitement of what choices are around the corner, of accepting your path as one of learnings and experiences, your vibration starts to rise.

Your whole life pattern for being here is to learn. You are constantly evolving to experience higher and higher states of love and higher states of vibration. Unfortunately, most of the vibrations that are experienced here on the earth plane are that of human labeling, needing, wanting, having, attaching to, owning, etc. That's not how true unconditional love works. However, how else will you be able to tell the difference if you don't experience the lower aspects of love for yourself?

Try this experiment next time you encounter an emotion that is heavy or uncomfortable. In that moment, do not judge it, for by judging it, you are only adding your own muck to the pile of muck. Do not label it. See the emotion for what it is. It is energy, pure and simple. Now ground it out (see Chapter Two on how to ground). Pay attention to your body. Feel yourself start to lighten up. Feel the heaviness flow through you and into the ground beneath your feet. Feel your own personal vibration start to rise.

By doing this simple exercise, you begin to learn what true unconditional love feels like. Keep doing this and you will find your own personal vibration continue to rise. Once you experience that, you will quickly discern what is high vibrational love and what isn't. And once you've touched the hem of that high vibrational love, there's no going back. Who would want to?

The lesson for you, therefore, is to realize you can ground out the muck. You can change the vibration of the muck. You don't need to get stuck on the treadmill of heavy human emotion. You don't need to continually plug into the drama. As an empath, you can take up the responsibilities of changing the energy around you. Yet you wouldn't even know about this responsibility if you hadn't been through your own spiritual boot camp.

Know that your soul wants to grow. With each lifetime, you get another opportunity to let your soul grow through the lessons you learn. Each lesson learned is another step up the ladder to ascension and enlightenment.

5

It Lasts Forever

Every thought, every emotion, every trauma that a human being has experienced since the beginning of time is out there in the ethers that surround us. As an empath, you have the responsibility of watching what you're putting out there because other empaths are feeling it. How can you use these situations as a powerful healing tool?

Albert Einstein once stated that time is not truly linear. It does, however, have an energetic vibration to it.

The energy of the past is heavier because it is full of our wants, our desires, our wills, and unrealized or unrequited loves or dreams that have already happened. We have loaded the past with our experiences, our thoughts, our energy. The energy of the future is lighter, however, because we don't know what will happen. Yes, we can also load up the future with what we'd like, but the truth is, we don't really know if what we desire will come to fruition. It is full of possibilities, not absolutes.

Or so we think.

Throughout our own experiences, we've discovered an astonishing fact that you may or may not accept. But we wouldn't be helping you if we didn't present it here.

There are those who believe that our lives are what we make of them. We make our own decisions, we live our lives on what we believe. We have free will and we make our choices based on that free will.

What if we were to tell you that the only free will you have is deciding when something will occur, not if it will occur.

This gets into the argument of whether you believe in predestination or if our lives are a crapshoot.

51

We'll give Alex a much-needed rest and present some illustrations from our own lives and you can decide for yourself.

From an early age, Steve dreamt of Uncle Sam. He'd sleep and see the man with the white beard and the red, white, and blue outfit pointing his finger at Steve and saying, "I Want You." Bewildered by the dreams, Steve wondered if maybe he was going to be called up for military service. Yet as he grew up and the dreams continued, he realized he wasn't going to war any time soon. So why the persistent dreams of Uncle Sam?

He lived his life, making decisions, exercising his free will that led him in a circuitous route through all sorts of situations and experiences. When he was in his mid-forties, he found himself with an unexpected opportunity to buy a nice piece of property that he could afford. He'd never given much thought to buying a house of his own, but the chance to own a small home on five acres in a picturesque town in New Hampshire was too good to turn down.

After moving in, he set out to explore his new town. To his astonishment, just three doors down from his new home, he discovered the childhood home of the man who later became the iconic figure of Uncle Sam.

He immediately looked up to the sky and asked, "How the hell did you know that no matter how much I screwed up my life, I was going to end up in this house?"

Doing further research into the history of Uncle Sam, other tidbits of information began to unfold. Uncle Sam's real name was Samuel Wilson – not too far a stretch from Steven Wilson. It also appeared, according to the historical records, that Samuel Wilson was a spy during the Revolutionary War, running covert messages to the Colonial troops. Steve remembered an incident that happened when he was in his twenties. He was visiting Faneuil Hall Marketplace in Boston, an area that has served as both a meetinghouse and marketplace since 1742. While walking through one of the oldest parts of the marketplace, he saw a man dressed as a British Redcoat. He was instantly seized with a panic so deep, he started to shake. His mind flooded with the need to get out of there – to escape and run away as far as he could. They're going to find me and capture me, repeated over and over in his head.

Could he have been picking up on the fact that Uncle Sam had been a spy, needing to stay as far away from the British as possible? Was this a coincidence? Or had he aligned to an energetic time line?

Bety too was busy living her life. Born in New York City, through a set of circumstances, she found herself living in New England by the time she was thirty. She was always spiritual by nature, but felt there was something lacking in her spiritual education. She'd met several teachers and learned many modalities, but still felt something was missing. In her professional career, she had an opportunity to leave a job she'd been at for several years. She believed this new job would be the job of a lifetime.

It turned out to be a nightmare.

Yet, through this nightmare, she learned several valuable lessons that helped in her journey as an empath. Still, the time came when she knew she had to leave. But where could she go?

Out of the blue, an opportunity fell into her lap that she didn't expect. A small New Age center was looking for someone to handle the financial and marketing responsibilities. The owner called Bety and offered her the position. The salary didn't come close to what she was making financially, but it was nevertheless an opportunity to leave the toxic situation she was in and, better still, work close to home. It was also one of those circumstances where she felt in every fiber of her being that taking this new job was the right thing to do.

It was at this New Age center where she met Steve and was so drawn to his world of shamanism that she began to study with him. Suddenly, everything opened up for her spiritually. This was the step she'd been missing all those years. It was as though everything she'd ever studied and done led her to this meeting with Steve. It was part of her path, part of her destiny to meet Steve and immerse herself in shamanism.

She didn't need to take the job at the New Age center. She didn't need to take the job that turned toxic. But the fact that her life has now expanded to the extent that it has demonstrates that it was preordained she meet Steve.

For Steve, he didn't need to buy the house that suddenly presented itself. He didn't need to start offering healings at the New Age center where he and Bety met. Their free wills dictated when it would happen, not if it would happen.

For both Steve and Bety, they were able to follow the next step in their lives by a simple process of staying in the present. By staying in the moment, they were able to experience what there was to experience right then. By experiencing what there was to experience right then, they were better able to follow the energy, follow what felt right and have it happen – for Steve, buying a house he'd been destined to buy since he was a child and for Bety, meeting the right teacher at the right moment.

Therefore, the challenge for any empath is to stay in the present – in the moment – and experience what there is to experience right now. Do you really want to put the heavier energy of the past into the future? Wouldn't you prefer to allow that which is meant to happen to occur on its own without your interference? As many of you have probably noticed, when you push something to happen before it's ready to happen, it inevitably blows up in your face. Or if you push for something to happen through your own will, it takes that much more of your personal energy to keep it going.

Many people are reluctant to admit there is a grand plan to their lives. They prefer to believe they have complete control over their destiny. However, we have found that indeed there is a plan to our existence. There are lessons to be learned, obstacles to overcome. Believe it or not, you choose what your experiences will be before you come into each life.

You choose who your parents will be, who your spouses will be. There is a particular lesson in each life that you are given an opportunity to learn and to heal, whether it's learning how to love, how to trust, how to appreciate yourself, and so on. Perhaps you chose an alcoholic parent because you needed to learn compassion. Perhaps you chose a spouse who would cheat on you because you needed to learn to value yourself more and not allow yourself to become a doormat.

As you go through your life, you draw these experiences to you so you can learn. Each event you get through makes you stronger, especially if you're an empath. Each obstacle you overcome, each lesson you learn brings you a peace of mind you would never experience if you'd run and hidden instead. The more you heal, the more freedom you experience within yourself as you release the burdens that hold you back and weigh you down.

By being in the moment and feeling the energy of that moment and following that energetic vibration, there is a magic that enters your life. We believe there is no such thing as coincidence. You are meant to meet the people you're meant to meet and experience the things you're meant to experience, according to the grand plan of your life. There is a vibration to it and, as an empath, you will feel that vibration. It will feel good, feel right. And since you acutely feel energy that feels good, as opposed to energy that feels not so good, you will invariably follow the good-feeling energy.

Having said all that, you will feel that time itself has an energetic vibration to it. How many of you have driven by those white crosses that are placed on highways at the sites of fatal accidents? These were placed there as memorials, but they also hold the energy of the traumatic deaths that occurred at each spot. As an empath, you will feel that traumatic energy whenever you drive by. Any battlefield, no matter where it is in the world, will retain the energy of the tragedies and trauma that took place there as well.

By experiencing and feeling all of this, you begin to understand that everything traumatic that has ever happened in the world has left an imprint. A sensitive person cannot help but feel it when they walk into that imprint of energy.

That's why grounding is so important. Once you learn to ground, you can go to these heavy-energy places. Rather than plug in and add your own emotions to an already energetically charged area, you can begin to ground out the energy and actually start to change its vibration. It will make you much more open to experiencing everything that is out there and not be afraid of it. As you begin to heal your own issues, you add your own light to an area and change its vibration. In effect, you will be the dishwasher soap that clears away the grime and dirt that is stuck in a heavy energetic place.

After Alex's revelation on how to move and change energy, he grew confident enough to start venturing out into the world more. He no longer feared that he wouldn't be able to deal with all the energies he was feeling. He developed a deeper interest in history and was no longer reluctant to visit places where tragedies or death had occurred.

One day, he went into an antique shop and, while looking around, was drawn to a glass frame that contained a cracked and very weather-beaten man's shoe mounted to it. As soon as he picked up the frame, he felt his stomach immediately lurch. He was filled with a deep sense of despair and terror. He felt so sick he thought he was going to vomit. Immediately, he put the item down and backed away as quickly as he could. Curious as to why he'd had such a reaction to an innocuous-looking object, he asked the owner of the antique shop what the item was. He was stunned when he was told it had been found in a German concentration camp.

Just as an empath can walk into a room and immediately feel if an argument has taken place or a traumatic event has occurred, they can also identify the energetic imprint that is retained in the items we own. Psychometry is the ability to pick up the energy from any given object and "read it," getting a sense of the person who owned it and the circumstances surrounding it.

The shoe in the antique shop had, in all probability, belonged to a victim of the Holocaust. By picking up the frame, Alex had experienced the person's fear, horror, utter helplessness, and despair. If a shoe can hold that much energy, imagine what a site where trauma has taken place on a monumental scale would feel like? Or an area where someone was murdered, or beaten, or abused? This is one of the reasons empaths fear their abilities. Without a foundational understanding of why they feel what they feel, and what they're supposed to do with these feelings, they experience the trauma, the sadness, the fear and despair, and take it on as their own.

The experience in the antique story led Alex to an awakening of his own psychic skills. The more he explored, the more fascinated he became. He read that each human being is surrounded by an aura. An aura is an energy field that surrounds all things. Everything that has ever happened (including situations from other lifetimes), as well as what will happen to humans, is all contained in their aura.

Alex began to experiment with reading the human aura. He saw colors that denoted where a person was at a particular stage in their life. Muddied or washed-out colors in any particular part of the aura showed an energy block or a potential illness. Bright colors showed the person had overcome a fear or block and was healthy in that particular area.

The human chakra system, which include energy points throughout the body, have particular colors associated with them. A person who can see the auric colors can read what chakra a person is struggling with or whether the chakra is healthy. For example, the heart chakra is green in color. A person who is loving, creative, communicative, or is a natural healer will have a bright green color in their aura surrounding their heart. However, if the green is dark or muddied, it indicates the person is closed off energetically or is struggling with image issues, such as low self-esteem, blaming others for their troubles, or deep-seated insecurity.

Becoming proficient at reading energy, Alex discovered there was a downside to all of this. His sharpened awareness gave him knowings of what a person would do before they did it or whether they would become ill. As a compassionate human being, he tried his best to fix the situation – prevent what was going to happen from taking place. He didn't realize that when he tried to do that, he ran the risk of interfering in someone's life path.

As difficult as it may sound to many of you, sometimes a person needs to become ill, or go through a traumatic event in order to learn a lesson from it. As an empath, you need to step back and look at the bigger picture. Did the person become ill because they were so busy taking care of others that they never took any time for themselves (thus becoming ill and forcing them now to take care of themselves)? Is a person getting into the same dysfunctional relationships because they haven't yet learned to value themselves?

It is only when we go through difficult times do we learn from them because many times, it isn't until we're hit over the head with a situation that we stop and try to figure out why it's happening and how we can stop it from happening again. At that moment is when a learning and an understanding takes place. If everything were taken care for us, we'd never learn.

By the same token, it makes you more aware of the energy you yourself put out. If places retain the energy of whatever happened, think of the energy angry or frightened people must have put out or may continue to put out. Think about the fear mongering that occurs every time you turn on the news. By getting pulled into the fear or the anger or the violence, you're only adding more fear, more anger, more violence to the mess.

There's a famous saying in the New Testament where Jesus tells his followers to turn the other cheek. For centuries, people have questioned this saying. Does this mean I have to become a doormat and let people walk all over me? What exactly did he mean by this? Whether you're a Christian or not, think about the saying for a moment from an energetic point of view.

For example, you are in the middle of an argument with your spouse. The words are becoming more heated, more violent. Your blood pressure is rising and you're beginning to lose control. What are you doing? You are adding more fuel to the fire. The energy you are putting out is of a lower frequency and it is igniting an already volatile situation. Now take the words "turn the other cheek" and apply it to this situation. In other words, pull back from the argument. Turn the other cheek energetically and stop feeding it with more negative energy. Take a deep breath and stop feeding each other the volatile energy. You will find that the argument will dissipate. Even if the other person continues, if you cease to feed it your energy, the other person will soon tire because they are expending their energy and not getting any of yours to replenish theirs.

When you turn the other cheek (remove your energy), the situation will in time grind to a halt. Now, if you replace the energy with calm, healing energy, and ground out the other person's anger, etc., you will soon see a change in the situation. You will have actually changed the energy of the situation.

This is the true path of an empath. It isn't to add more dysfunctional energy to an already dysfunctional world. It is to take that energy and change its vibration. The only way to learn how to do this and understand how energy works and why, is to live through each situation – experience every experience. Experiment with the energy. And know that everything you put out stays there. That's how an empath can walk into any area where something traumatic has taken place and feel that energy. That's how Alex was able to feel the energy from the shoe he picked up. That's how we know when someone is down, or happy, or sad. We feel it.

REMOVING THE MUCK

Everything that has ever happened, or will happen – good, bad, or indifferent – has an energy to it. This is what an empath feels. You need to understand the energy you're leaving behind or are creating in the moment whether it's in a relationship, a job, etc. As you do the inner work and begin to heal, your energy becomes higher. You become a better manifestor as your ability to know and sense truth or an untruth increases. However, because your energy is higher, the imprint you leave behind is stronger. And because it's higher, part of your responsibility as an empath is to make sure your imprint is there to help add more light to a situation or a person. There's more than enough muck in the world right now. Our responsibility is to remove the muck as best we can, starting with ourselves.

6

It Is What It Is

You can drive yourself crazy trying to figure out why you are feeling what you are feeling and whether it has a particular meaning. Many times it means nothing; it's just an experience of energy, which adds to the "tool box" of knowledge for you to learn how energy works.

If there is one consistency among human beings, it's that we all want to fall in love. Think of the euphoric feelings you get when you're in love. It's almost as though you're walking on air and time speeds up. The time you spend with your beloved never seems to be enough. Why does this happen? Because it feels so good energetically.

As an empath, who feels everything deeply already, this feeling of being in love is really going to hit you. And because it feels so good, you're going to do everything in your power to keep it going.

Empaths learn at a young age what good energy feels like and try everything they can to hold onto that. They seek out those situations, or those people in their lives who will continue to make them feel good.

Who hasn't met a person whom we thought was right for us, only to have the relationship blow up in our faces? How many times have you tried to change a person or change a situation in the interests of trying to help another, because by helping and changing them, you feel good?

One of the most important lessons to learn is that you cannot change anyone who doesn't want to change. No matter how hard you try, it just isn't going to happen. And here's something else to consider: empaths tend to hold onto relationships they should have let go of long ago because, in the moment when they feel love, it becomes the goal of the relationship. They will turn themselves into pretzels to keep that love going. However, many times the love they are feeling is their own projection of what they need bouncing back to them, especially from someone who, for whatever reason, cannot love them back.

Remember, a large part of being an empath is that you will be presented with scenarios that allow you to feel all kinds of energy. The important thing to understand is that in many of these scenarios, you will not be able to change anything. If you've done your own inner work and your vibration is high, you will offer another the opportunity to choose which way they want to go – whether they too want to heal and walk in their truth, or continue to live with their issues and fears. It will be up to them, not you.

If you haven't done the work and are constantly trying to manipulate or change a situation or a person, it will eventually fail and you will continue to be presented with a similar situation or person until you learn that all you can do is accept the situation or the person for what they are and move on if necessary.

Acceptance is probably the hardest thing for a human being, and especially an empath, to learn. We think we can change a person only to find out, painfully, that we cannot. We have to look at the bigger picture. A person is going through whatever they are going through because they have their own lessons to learn. Many times they are in situations through their own choices. By you trying to take that lesson away, by perhaps becoming an enabler, no matter how altruistic you think you're being, you are actually being detrimental to that person's growth. By the same token, you have to accept that not everyone is "going to get it." You have to be okay with that. We've all been guilty of giving advice and guidance to others, only to have them completely ignore us. Why? Because they have to experience it for themselves. Just as you've had to experience your own trials and tribulations.

All of us have met people who irritate or bother us. They have a way of pushing your buttons. Rather than getting upset, try taking a step back. Why are they pushing your buttons? Why are you getting angry, or upset, or hurt?

Because there's an issue that you haven't healed.

As crazy as it sounds, these people are actually doing you a favor by revealing there's a button still within you that needs to be healed. You are the only one who can heal it. Unfortunately, there are no magic pills or potions that will do the healing for you. Mainstream or holistic energy healers can only give you the tools to help you heal yourself.

Until you heal a particular issue, you will continue to attract those people to you who will continue to push that button. However, the good news is that once you heal the issue and "remove the button," you will know it because the next time a similar situation happens, you will not react the way you once did. Rather than react with anger or hurt, which are lower vibrational energies, you will now react with compassion and non-judgment, which are higher vibrational energies. You will no longer leak your own energy by reacting in an adverse manner. You will start to see that the person who is a bully or miserable or miserly picked a difficult life path for themselves because of the lessons they need to learn. As we said earlier, they may learn it, they may not. All you can do is honor them for the onerous path they picked to walk in this life. As for you, the way you react to any given situation will tell you whether you've learned your lesson.

On another note, how many things in your life have you felt this irresistible pull towards, as if everything had to take a backseat, even though it may not have been in your interests or even detrimental to your health? When people are stressed, they reach for sweets, food, cigarettes, alcohol. Or they buy things they don't need because it makes them feel good at the moment they're buying it. Understanding how and why this happens is huge because it will free you from anything that can be perceived as addicting, or a pull on your energy. It brings you autonomy from all those things which would taint or pollute your personal energy.

So it was with Alex. As you can see in prior chapters, many of his journeys were about how people made him feel or why certain behaviors weren't comfortable in his body. He was learning to witness how he reacted to these situations and to change the way he looked at things. Was he being judgmental? Negative?

Throughout all of this, he was also working on not slipping into a "me versus them" mentality. He learned that nothing would drain his energy more than getting into an adversarial energetic pattern, whether it be with other humans or through his own fears.

When Alex got into high school, he began to notice girls. Like his peers, he had a deep need and desire to have a girlfriend. Yet he was hampered by self-doubts. Could he be loved? Was he so weird, so "out there" because of his deep emotional feelings that no one would ever go out with him?

The lesson of needing to be validated in love was about to unfold.

Because of the band, Alex knew he could have as many women as he wanted. But he didn't want casual sex. He wanted to experience a rich, loving relationship that meant something to both parties. He tried his best to connect, on a deeper level, with the opposite sex. There were more misses than hits. But when he finally did meet that special girl, it was as though the floodgates opened. He felt a warmth, a physical love so profound he couldn't put words to it. He was determined to hold onto this relationship because it made him feel so good, so wanted, so validated that he was capable of being loved. Yet as the relationship progressed in its natural ebbs and flows, Alex grew fearful. Was she pulling away from him? Was she being more attentive? Did she really care about him? Each time he slipped into that insecurity, he lost sight of the bigger picture, the lesson that was unfolding.

After a few months, the attentiveness began to wane. That first flush of excitement disappeared. Alex worried and fretted. How could he keep this going? Was it something he was doing that was making her pay less attention to him? He tried harder. He rearranged himself, tried different things. He began to bargain away who he was. This need, this desire, this feeling of love was too overwhelming to let go of.

Despite his herculean efforts, the relationship fell apart. Alex found himself in a quandary. What could he have done to fix this? Was there still something he could do to resurrect this relationship that had felt so good, so fulfilling?

Alas, there was no fix. His heart shattered into a million pieces, but he kept trying. He had to or else, in his own mind, he would cease to exist. He did all those things men do in order to hold on. He became a stranger to himself. Unfortunately, the girl was ready to move on. In the end, he had no choice but to let her go.

Licking his wounds in the privacy of his bedroom, Alex tried to figure out what had happened. What was it about the feelings brought up in the relationship that made him feel so purposeful? Was it something he did that caused its demise? Did he have to become better? Stronger?

The lesson continued.

After grieving the loss of this relationship, which had been so monumental to Alex, he continued on with his life. Soon, another relationship presented itself. Once again, he did the same things he'd done with the first. He tried to be the person he thought the girl wanted so she would love him. Once again, it faded away as quickly as it started. He suffered another broken heart, another crisis of the soul. Was he just not lovable? Was he meant to be alone the rest of his life?

This continued off and on until he was in college. Relationships started with the best of intentions, only to inevitably blow up in his face. Through each relationship, he tried his best to be everything he believed the girl needed or wanted. It never seemed to be enough.

Finally, after another relationship fiasco, he found himself alone in his dorm room. He turned off the lights and prayed that he be given the answer to his dilemma. What was he doing wrong? What could he do to change his dismal history of relationships? He needed to understand what was going on. Slipping into the dreamtime, he found himself in a cold, forbidding monastery. There was no light, no sensations. It was devoid of emotion.

Sitting in a tiny cell with only a cot to keep him company, he suddenly heard a voice fill the room.

"Who do you serve?" the voice asked.

Alex thought about it for a moment. "I serve love, I suppose, because it makes me feel good inside. It makes me feel comfortable. It makes me feel worthy."

"How are you validated by this love?" the voice asked again.

Alex shrugged. "I'm validated because it makes me feel good," he repeated. "I feel perfect when I'm in love. When she loves me back, I feel validated."

Once again, the voice said, "How do you know this to be so if you are serving yourself?"

At that moment, Alex awoke. His dream left him perplexed. Is that what he'd been doing? In his need to feel that energy of love, to be validated by another person, had he truly been serving just himself? What exactly did that mean?

He put the dream aside and went about his day. Realizing he needed groceries, he went to the local supermarket. As he walked down the aisles, he began to notice a discomfort creep up on him. This was strange. He'd been in this supermarket countless times and never felt this uneasiness.

Stopping in the bakery section, he picked up a bag of chocolate brownie cookies. They were his favorite and he never gave up an opportunity to buy them. This time, however, when he picked up the bag, he suddenly felt as though he were holding a 100-pound brick. He looked at the date on the bag. They were freshly baked that day. He put the bag down and instantly felt better.

"What the hell?" he whispered under his breath.

He picked up another bag of cookies – this time chocolate chip. The same heaviness overcame him. When he put them down, the heaviness instantly disappeared. He stood in the aisle and pondered what was going on. He checked in with his body and realized that when he put the bag of cookies down, he felt a lightness in his being, as if he and the cookies were completely separate in the moment. He was more empowered.

Huh, he thought to himself. This is beyond weird. Still, the chocolate brownie cookies were his favorite. They were his comfort food. They'd always made him feel good in the past, especially if he'd had a trying day. Despite the strange energetic experience, he went ahead and bought them.

Arriving at home, he slowly unpacked the grocery bags. As he did so, he paid close attention to how each item made him feel. He held the carton of vegetables, the bag of grapes. He held the package of ground beef and pasta noodles. Each item he held made him feel inexplicably heavy. Yet as soon as he let them go, he felt light. A light bulb went off in his head. I feel this way when I'm with people. When I'm by myself, I feel light. When I get around others, I feel heavy.

By way of a test, he opened up the bag of cookies and ate one. As soon as he did, the heaviness went into his body. He no longer felt light; no longer felt as though he were in charge. He felt drained. He no longer enjoyed the taste of the chocolate brownie cookie, no longer felt the comfort it had once brought him.

Okay, just what the heck was going on here?

As he'd done countless times in the past, when he went to bed that night, he asked for clarification. What are you trying to teach me? What am I missing here?

He fell asleep and instantly found himself in an apple orchard. Before him stood a beautiful, shimmering tree. Sunshine shone down upon the tree, lighting up the golden apples hanging from its branches. Looking down at the base of the tree, he had a sense of its roots digging deep into the earth, enriching itself with both the nutrients of the soil and the richness of the sunshine. It was healthy, bountiful and glowing with a wondrous energy. It was as though the sun, the earth, and the energy were all working together in harmony to produce the best fruit possible. He stepped up to the tree and plucked one of the apples from a low-hanging branch. Biting into it, he was suddenly infused with a love so pure, so unaffected, he had nothing to compare it with. He felt the light of the sunshine flow into him. He felt his feet connect more to the earth. He physically felt the magic of nature operating in partnership to produce the apples: the sun kissing the apples, the soil reaching up through the trunk of the tree and enveloping the fruit in its nurturing arms. It was so perfect, so peaceful.

The dream shifted.

He now found himself in another orchard. There before him was another tree, with another full bounty of apples. As they hung from the branches, they too were bathed in the same golden light as the first apple tree. However in this orchard, there were workers picking the apples and placing them in long wooden crates. The men were tired and miserable. It had been a long day. They were sweating profusely in the hot sun. Many just wanted to get this task over with so they could go home. Alex noticed their energy and emotions flowing into the apples.

He watched as the foreman approached. He too was tired and flustered.

"Hurry up!" the foreman barked at the workers. "We have a quota to meet and you're not picking fast enough. Fill up those boxes now or else you're fired!"

Alex saw the workers' frustrated and angry reactions mingle with the foreman's surly emotions. Together, this energy flowed into the apples. The golden light that had once surrounded the apples grew dim and muddied as the lower vibrational energy from the workers and foreman suffused the fruit.

The scene shifted once more. Now he was standing in the office of the orchard's owner. The man was at his desk, pouring over the ledgers, adding up the columns to see if his orchard was making enough money. He ticked the figures, grumbling aloud about the need to fire some of the workers. They weren't working fast enough. He wanted more out of them. This orchard wasn't a charity. He'd bought it to make money. Lots of it. All these thoughts and emotions found their way into the apples as well.

Now Alex found himself in his supermarket, standing in the aisle, holding the bag of chocolate brownie cookies he'd bought.

He abruptly awoke. And started to think. The conclusion he came to hit him hard. He knew people sent out thoughts and feelings. Heck, he felt them every day. Was it possible this energy also collected in the foods we ate? Was what he'd felt holding the cookies in the supermarket a bigger interaction of energy than he'd ever imagined?

Later that week, too lazy to cook, he decided to stop off at the local pizzeria for dinner. Walking in, he was immediately struck by how cute the girl behind the counter was. With her long, red hair and honey-hazel eyes, she was a knock-out.

Ordering a sandwich, he told her just how he liked it made. She smiled at him, giving him an opening to pursue a conversation. They flirted and laughed and he felt his energy change. The more she flirted back, the more his energy shifted. As she made his sandwich, he saw, to his delight, that the energy of her attentiveness to him, her perception of him as a young man she'd like to get to know better was pouring into the sandwich. He had an "a-ha" moment.

What I'm learning about food is even bigger than I thought, he realized. When someone cares, that energy goes into the food. When they don't care, a lesser energy goes in and I'm eating it.

Alex took the sandwich and went home. While eating it, he was amazed by how wonderful it tasted. Was it the ingredients or the energy the girl had put into it while she was making the sandwich that made it taste so good?

There was, however, another side to this situation. Because of his fondness for the girl, he was drawn to the pizzeria. He couldn't help himself. On one level, he knew she was too pretty for him. Although she'd been sweet and flirty, he didn't think she'd actually go out with him. Despite his growing reputation as a musician, he still wasn't so well known that everyone, including the girl at the pizzeria, would instantly recognize him. Yet on another level, that sandwich had tasted so good. He began to experience the pull, the desire to go back. It was so strong, he knew he had to follow through on it.

He made himself wait a few days before returning to the pizzeria. This time the girl was on her cellphone. She was arguing and obviously very upset. Ordering his sandwich, he watched as she made it while still quarreling on the phone. No love or attentiveness was going into the sandwich that day. At the same time he noticed her energy going into the sandwich, he felt his own thwarted needs and desires going into the sandwich as well. His pull, his desire, his declaration that the return visit to the pizzeria would be good for him, his need to be validated by this girl, all went into the sandwich.

He paid for the sandwich and slunk out of the pizzeria. When he got home, he began to beat himself up. Why did he ever think she'd be interested in him? How could he think this beautiful girl would make his life happy? That she was the one he'd been searching for? How could he have been so foolish? His vibration plunged the more he castigated himself. Taking the sandwich out of the bag, his desire to eat it was gone. He realized at that moment that he never, ever wanted to feel that way again.

For the next week, he made sure to keep to himself. He had no desire to get pulled into any interpersonal relationships with anyone. It just wasn't worth it. However, the way of the empath won't allow this situation to go on. If one avenue of comfort is cut off, the empath will find another, even if it's with people. They will find some way or some person to fill them up and validate them and bring them comfort.

As Alex resisted getting plugged into people, other physical things in his life began to pull him in more deeply in order to fill the hole within himself that wanted and needed validation. People weren't doing it. But drinking and smoking did, at least for a little while. However, because it's a false grounding (not rooted in true energy from Source), it never lasted and he had to drink and smoke more to keep filling that hole up. It got to a point where he felt himself losing control over his life. Once again, he asked his guidance to help him figure it all out.

In the dreamtime, they took him back to the apple orchard. He experienced again the sunshine pouring into the tree, the love and light flowing into the apples. He saw everything working in perfect unison to bring forth the fruit on the branches. He was then shown the second orchard with the unhappy workers, the nasty foreman, the money-hungry owner. These apples didn't have the same connection to the earth as the first tree did. It was as if the apples were incomplete in some way. As if something or someone were interfering in their unison with the sun and the earth. The dysfunctional energy of the people interacting with the apples had broken the tie of the journey of the apple.

He saw these apples sitting in their boxes – forlorn, lifeless. No love, no light surrounding them. Yet people were clamoring for these apples. If they didn't eat these apples, they felt they wouldn't be happy. Someway, somehow, they felt validated by these apples and needed more and more of them to keep the validation going and feel happy within themselves.

When Alex awoke, he was more confused than ever. Just once, he grumbled, I wish Guidance would tell me in plain English what I need to know!

He courageously made his way back to the pizzeria, back to the pretty girl, back to the object of his affections, back to someone who'd made him feel good. This time when he arrived, she wasn't arguing on the phone. But it was obvious she's wasn't in a good place energetically. Alex thought to himself, maybe I can use my empathy to help her. If I'm clever and successful enough, this will show her I care. Maybe then she may consider going out with me.

"Hey, what's up? You seem kinda down."

She flicked a strand of red hair over her shoulder. "My boss wants me to work this weekend."

"Is that so bad?"

"This week has been a week from hell. I just wanted to de-stress and go out with my friends. They're going to a concert with one of my favorite bands. I'm telling you, if I don't go, I'll just die!"

"Can't someone fill in for you?"

She shook her head. "I tried to get someone to cover, but everybody has plans."

"What if you just went to this concert anyway?"

"Guaranteed to get me fired. And I need the money. Any way you look at it, I'm totally screwed."

Speaking to Alex, the girl's energy changed. As her energy changed, so did his. Her story became his story. Her need and desire to go to the concert wasn't being allowed to happen. His own need and desire to be with this girl wasn't being allowed to happen.

"Can you go some other time to see your band?" he asked.

"No. It has to be this time."

Alex felt his body inexplicably clench. To his surprise his feet began to ache. His heart hurt. He mentally took a step back. What was going on? What was he supposed to learn at that moment?

"Well," he replied. "The world has a way of working things out. What's important will make its way to you."

She sighed. "I don't believe that. Things never work out for me. It always goes wrong."

As she said this, his stomach became tighter. He thought he was going to be sick. Before that happened, he quickly paid for his sandwich and left.

By the time he arrived home, he noticed his stomach felt better. The pain in his heart had subsided and his feet no longer ached.

Alex thought back to his initial dream with the monastery. It had been devoid of energy, devoid of life. It was cold and forbidding. There was nothing feeding it. There was no harmony in its existence.

In that instant, the answer clicked. Was he looking for that harmony, that unison, that perfect apple somewhere else? Was he, in his eagerness to attain validation, getting in his own way? Was the love and light that had poured into the first apple supposed to come from that place of love and light? Not from each other, not from things outside of himself, but from a higher source? The same source that gifted the first apple?

He recalled the first apple had not been interfered with in any way. The fulfilling light of the sun had been allowed to come down and enter the apple. The strength of the earth had been allowed to come up the trunk of the tree and enter the fruit. There was no one – no people, no workers, no orchard owners – no one to intrude and put their own energies and intentions into the apple. That's why it had felt and tasted so good. The other apple, on the contrary, had been meddled with. All the people who had come in contact with the second apple filled it with their own unhappiness, their own worries, their own intentions. By the time it got to the store, the energy of the apple was so dreadful, its taste reflected that.

Alex sat and mulled this over. It made so much sense to him, especially when he remembered the girl in the pizzeria. The first sandwich she'd made for him tasted so good because she'd been filling the sandwich with her attentiveness to him. However, the subsequent sandwiches never reached that wholesome taste because she'd been angry or depressed or just not in a good place. He too had contributed to the taste of the sandwich by pouring his own wants and needs into it instead of just allowing the sandwich to be a sandwich, without interference, without intention.

In that moment, Alex realized he didn't need to be validated by things and people outside himself. Just like the first apple, he allowed himself to be filled with the light and fullness of energy from a higher Source; a Source that wasn't interfered with by human emotions or intentions. The love that poured into him was so profound, so indescribable, so pure that he began to cry.

When you begin to understand how the world works energetically, you stop validating yourself with things and people outside yourself. All these things and people actually interfere in the process of filling yourself up with the energy and love from a higher place because these things and people fill you up with their own intentions, their own energies, their own thought processes, which, many times, is not coming from a higher source.

Empathic people, in particular, crave validation so deeply, they'll do all sorts of things to get it, whether it's bargaining themselves away, changing how they look, behaving any way they need to. However, this only attracts lower vibrational energy to them because it's not based in truth. In their minds, bad energy is better than no energy. Eventually, it gets to a point where this lower vibrational energy doesn't serve them anymore.

When it comes to relationships, we go into it needing to experience a particular energy – a feeling that we can love and be loved. But the majority of relationships can't sustain that feeling of love because it's based on a false premise. Many people unknowingly fall in love because the other person "completes them," "makes them feel safe," etc. What if you don't need that? True love doesn't come from outside yourself. True love comes from within. When we, as empaths, learn our energetic lessons, our energy changes. We stand in the truth of who we are. What kind of person do you think you'd attract then? As "like energy attracts like energy," you will attract someone who can truly nourish you, someone who doesn't ask you to change who you are to suit them, someone who doesn't burden you with their own insecurities and neediness and demands. Just as you allow them to be themselves, so they do to you. You become like the first apple. You have learned to get out of your own way. You've learned to allow the higher energies of love and energy to flow through you. You become the physical embodiment of that pure love. Instead of living in a constant state of needing to be validated, living in empathic victimhood, you become the example of another way of being. Another message that can be brought forth into a world that is negative and self-absorbed.

By way of illustration, let's turn back to Alex. As a musician, Alex naturally attracted a lot of women. Yet the relationships he pursued always seemed to have a common thread running through them. While Alex gave everything he had to make the relationship work, the women were so consumed with their own issues, they were unable to return his love. Over and over again this happened. Being an empath, Alex felt the implosion of these relationships deeply. He wondered if he wasn't doing enough, wasn't giving enough. He began to take on full responsibility each time a relationship ended.

Finally, when yet another relationship imploded, he took a hard look at his history with women. Why was it that he continually attracted women who were incapable of loving him back? Why did he give everything he had to make it work and still have it fall apart? What was the message here that he was obviously missing? Then it hit him.

He wasn't surrendering.

In other words, he wasn't accepting the plain, unvarnished truth that he couldn't change these women. And because he hadn't realized he couldn't change them, he kept attracting the same type of woman to himself over and over again in order to teach him this vital and painful lesson.

We have seen this scenario over and over again. Books have been written about this. People think they can change their partner, mold them into whatever they need for themselves. It never works. Because if you try to change yourself for another, you're not walking in the truth of who you are. And if you try to change someone else, you're not allowing them to walk in the truth of who they are. Nor are you allowing them to go through whatever they need to go through to learn whatever lessons they need to learn.

There are also those people who, when the euphoric first blush of love wears off and the true work begins of meshing two different people into a viable, working relationship, they take off. They can't deal with the fact that relationships take work. They find flaws in their partners because they're not measuring up to what the person's image of what they believe true love is. They fail to see that they are living their life wearing rose-colored glasses. They are trying to mold people to their unrealistic expectations without allowing the person to be who they are.

We all love those romantic movies or novels where everything gets tied up in a red bow and the couple walk off into the sunset, living happily ever after. Unfortunately, these books and movies have done a disservice to us. It's made us believe that our relationships will be perfect. That we'll meet that special one, instantly fall in love, and never have to compromise or work at the relationship.

Then there are those relationships where one spouse pours all their energy into the relationship to make it work, while the other spouse only takes. In a balanced relationship, both partners give and take. Their energies ebb and flow with each other. However, when one spouse is constantly giving away their energy, they run the risk of becoming ill because they are giving themselves away trying to make the other person happy, trying to keep things on an even keel. As we stated in an earlier chapter, we get our energy from Source. We shouldn't be taking it from others or giving it away to the extent that we deplete ourselves and become ill in the process.

For better or worse, it is what it is. Every relationship gives us an opportunity to learn much about ourselves. To feel all the different emotions there are to feel in such an intimate situation. To know the difference between feeling authentic love from another person, or just your own projection of what you want to feel. It's not easy to do this. But if you have the courage to look hard at your relationships and see them in the light of day and surrender to the truth of what they are, you have a better chance of feeling an energy that is real. All of this serves as a teacher, an experience, an opportunity to see the higher truth. To live an authentic life.

It is what it is and you don't need to do anything to change that.

BECOMING TRANSPARENT

There are many things in life that we're drawn to, whether it's people, situations, or physical stimulants. One of the most beautiful gifts of empathy is the ability to witness your experience. You receive many clues from your surroundings. You feel in your body, you sense things other people don't pick up on. In the dreamtime, you are given much knowledge. You understand why these things happen, why you are drawn to certain people, situations, etc. There's the potential for change. For learning. For removing false barriers to your life. However, if you shut things out that make you uncomfortable and don't allow yourself to witness and experience, your journey comes to a halt. Just as the second apple in our analogy above, the apple (and you) never finish your job. You are interfered with, many times by yourself. Stop a moment and ask yourself why you are feeling what you feeling or sensing what you're sensing. Begin to discern the truth of what is really going on in any given situation. Don't allow your own fears, pre-conceived thought processes or others' thoughts to interfere with your journey.

You cannot force situations, or force people to change. You can't hide from whatever energies they are projecting at you. If you do hide, you'll only find another person who will do the exact same thing. However, you can re-learn how to react to it. Grounding is one way. Yet there is another way. We call it becoming transparent.

Think of how an ice cube is created. When you slow down water molecules, they become dense and cold. Soon they harden into a cold substance we call ice. The human body is mostly made of water. Now what do you think happens when the energy within us stops flowing? For example, judging a person will slow the vibration of your energy in that moment. You own or take on the energy of whatever the other person is thinking and projecting at you in that moment. Your energy begins to slow and creates a block within you.

Many empaths suffer from physical and psychosomatic pain because the energy isn't moving through them. Why? Because, like ice, it has become dense in your own body. Yet what happens when you get the energy moving? Like ice, it melts and things begin to flow again. If you, as an empath, begin to allow people to be who they are and allow them and the situation to be what it is, you become transparent. There's no density in your body for their energies to stick to. Try it next time you come up against a person or an uncomfortable situation. Don't judge it, don't own it. Simply see it for what it is and allow the energy to move right through you. If you do find yourself reacting adversely, then you know this is something you need to look at within yourself – something you still need to heal.

On another note, in this chapter, we mentioned food and how empaths react to certain things they eat. As with everything else, our food is filled with the energy of the people who handle it. Could this be the basis for much of the food allergies that are popping up? Could people, especially sensitive ones, be reacting more to the energy being put into their foods, including the trauma of the animals when they are slaughtered, rather than the food itself? Food for thought.

7

Simultaneous Time

An empath can feel and access the past, present, and future, sometimes all at the same time. Why does this happen and how can you deal with such a situation?

Albert Einstein, one of the most profound experts on energy, once wrote the following statement about time, "Physicists believe the separation between past, present, and future is only an illusion, although a convincing one."

He and many of his colleagues believed that past, present, and future are all happening simultaneously. Right now, at this very moment.

This is how shamans are able to access the past, present, and future to do the various types of healings they perform, such as soul retrievals and past trauma relief. Everything we have ever gone through in every life we have ever lived remains in our auric field, including injuries and physical and emotional traumas.

Every aspect of our existence has an energetic vibration to it. Every thought, every word, every intention, every emotion, every action has an energy attached to it. Add to that every life ever lived, every memory, every injury or trauma ever suffered. Because an empath is acutely sensitive to energy, they sometimes experience what we call a jump in time. It's the ability to suddenly find themselves reliving a moment or an emotion that is not of the present, but from the past. At first it is incredibly unnerving, until you begin to understand why it happens and how it can be used as an incredibly powerful healing tool.

When Alex was five years old, the world turned upside down. Literally.

His family had moved to a new town in New England. It was one of those lovely summer days, when the sky was a deep blue and there wasn't a cloud to be seen. He was playing in his sandbox with his toy soldiers. Like many young boys, he'd always been intrigued by battles and war. His toy soldiers were his prized possessions and they went everywhere with him. It wasn't until later in life that he would realize why he loved those soldiers so much.

However, on this particular day, he had no thoughts of empathy or psychic abilities or the spiritual adventures that would await him. He was busy setting up a battle in the cool sand, positioning his soldiers in fight formation. Suddenly, he heard a low hum. He looked around, but saw nothing that could be giving off such an ominous sound. And it was ominous, though he had no idea why. The humming grew louder. His heartbeat increased. His mouth went dry. He knew he shouldn't look up into the sky. The answer was there, yet he didn't want to know it. Still, as the hum increased, his curiosity got the better of him. He peeked up into the sky...and began to scream.

Where a moment before the sky had been a beautiful blue, it was now filled with thousands of black triangles flying overhead. Whether they were truly there or not, in that instant, they were Alex's reality. His panic grew.

"They're coming to get us again! They're coming to get us again!" Hysterical with fear, he jumped up and ran to the only place he felt safe at that time in his life – his grandmother's house, which was located next door to his.

Dashing inside, he threw himself on the floor and tried to put his feet on the ceiling because he felt the world around him turning upside down. His mother and grandmother tried to calm him, not understanding what he was trying to tell them. They went outside and pointed up to the sky. There were no black triangles. No one was trying to get him. The world was not turning upside down. Yet the terror of seeing those triangles and the sensation of trying to physically right himself were so overwhelming, it took him nearly an hour to finally calm down.

The family worried – not because of what he'd seen, but for more mundane reasons. Unable to understand what he'd been through, the incident was swept under the rug and never discussed again. Alex learned not to speak of it, and the memories were carefully filed away.

Life went on.

When he was eleven, he fell out of a tree and was seriously injured. Being rushed to the hospital, his family was told he'd have to undergo surgery. The operation was performed and hours later, Alex regained consciousness in the hospital room. He was alone, hooked up to various machines through IV tubes.

For no apparent reason, he found himself staring at the wall opposite the bed. It was a white wall with nothing distinguishable about it. Yet, to his shock, the wall suddenly turned into a big wooden door. The door slowly opened, revealing what looked like the Roman Coliseum coming into focus. Was this a movie he was watching? But there was no projector, no screen. Simply an arena where the wall had once been.

He heard the sounds of people cheering. He smelled the sand and felt the heat of the day. A movement to his right caught his attention. He looked and once again he felt the same horror he'd felt in the sandbox all those years before overcome him. However, this time, instead of seeing black triangles, he watched as his mother, grandmother, and sister were marched out into the middle of the arena by Roman soldiers and tied to wooden poles. A moment later lions were released and he saw his family ripped to pieces by the wild animals. Once again, what he was seeing became his reality. As far as he was concerned, what he was witnessing was happening at that very moment. He started screaming and yelling at the top of his lungs for them to stop. Ripping the IVs out of his arms, he ran out into the hallway. It took the doctors and nurses several minutes to calm him down and return him to his bed. His behavior was chalked up to a bad reaction to the anesthesia.

When Alex was sixteen, he found himself at an air show. Looking back, he realized how strange it was that he would end up at such an event. His family had no interest in planes, nor had they ever expressed a desire to go to an air show. But what the family didn't know was Alex's growing obsession with military planes – specifically a P-47 Thunderbolt. He'd read everything he could on the plane, making toy models and drawing endless pictures of them. He discovered that the P-47 Thunderbolt was the largest, heaviest and most expensive fighter-bomber in history to be powered by a single piston engine. It had four 50-caliber machine guns per wing and was particularly successful at ground attack during World War II, both in Europe and in the Pacific.

Now here he was, face-to-face with the plane that had obsessed him for years. As he stood in front of the plane, he shifted into another reality. He watched himself sitting in the cockpit of the plane. He watched himself attempting to evade enemy fire, maneuvering the heavy plane for all it was worth. He then watched the plane get hit and go down in a ball of fire with him still at the controls. It took all his willpower not to scream out in horror as he watched his own terrible death.

By the time he was thirty, Alex had experienced similar instances of reliving a moment in time. Watching a film about Waterloo, he instantly became overwhelmed with emotion when he realized a decision he'd made had caused the senseless slaughter of his men. And what was this obsession with extra-terrestrials? Why were these things happening over and over again? What was going on? Yet it took two more events to make him realize it was time to figure it all out.

One day Alex found himself participating in a service at a local spiritualist church. Many empaths are drawn to the spiritualist church because of its tradition of deep mysticism and strong belief in life after death. In the middle of the service, a middle-aged woman entered the small church. Alex had never seen her before and casually thought she was simply late for service. However, to his surprise, she walked down the aisle and planted herself in front of him. Digging into the deep recesses of her oversized sweater, she took out a piece of paper and thrust it at him.

"What are these? You're the only one who knows. You must remember."

Alex's first thought was that the woman was crazy and he slowly tried to move away from her. However, she was insistent and once again thrust the small piece of paper in his face. Reluctantly, Alex took it and glanced down at it. He caught his breath when he saw she had drawn a crude black triangle.

A short time after, while attending a flea market, he was strolling down a long lane of sellers, hoping to find a crystal to add to his growing collection. Suddenly, he felt a pair of hands on his shoulders and before he knew what was happening, he was swung around. He found himself facing a short, rotund black woman, dressed in Caribbean clothing. She cocked her head at him and smiled. "They're coming back, you know. What are we going to do about it?"

By now Alex knew these occurrences were not happenstance. He strongly believed there was no coincidences. So what were these triangles all about? What were these women trying to tell him?

Throughout his experiences up to this point, Alex knew that if he waited long enough, an answer would present itself. So he waited.

One evening, about a month after the strange encounters, he was flipping through the channels on his TV when an image immediately caught his attention.

It was the black triangle!

Raising the volume, he watched, mesmerized as the show spoke of whether alien life had found its way to our world. To his astonishment, the show claimed there have been many sightings, paintings, and carvings of the triangular objects hovering in the sky, whether in the American Southwest, Europe, or South America.

When the show was over, Alex sat back on his couch and mulled over the last few months. How had these women known to search Alex out? It was impossible they would have known of his experiences in his sandbox so many years before. Was there something, some energy, they sensed in him the way he was able to sense energy in others? Was it conceivable that he was somehow part of their energetic time line?

He had no answers. Not yet, anyway. But he knew the experiences weren't over.

He was right.

It was early summer and he was wandering through the streets of Salem, Massachusetts. At this point in his life, Alex had become interested in esoteric subjects, specifically Wiccan, and he'd spent the day popping into the various book and retail stores to find out what he could about the earth-based religion. As he walked down the street, an elderly woman seemingly came out of nowhere and abruptly stopped in front of him.

"You know," she said with a smile. "Someday the earth is going to turn upside down again. Some are going to fall off and some are going to stay on." She laughed uproariously before turning on her heel and disappearing down the street, never to be seen again. Alex was stunned. The memory of his experience in the sandbox came roaring back. It had happened more than thirty years before, yet this woman somehow knew about it. How? And, more specifically, why?

In that moment, standing on the sidewalk on that warm summer day, it suddenly started to make sense to Alex. What if this had happened before? What if all those strange things he'd experienced since the age of five were events he'd actually lived through? What if something was deliberately triggering these memories?

Yet, what was the meaning behind it all?

Alex threw himself into researching the question of the world turning upside down. In the library, he stumbled across a book about Edgar Cayce. Known as the "sleeping prophet," Cayce was able, through a self-induced sleep, to connect with time and space and give readings regarding all manner of topics. Alex was fascinated to discover that Cayce spoke about the Earth's poles shifting. According to Cayce, the poles had shifted in the past and there was speculation they would shift again.

Delving further, he found writings on the ancient prophecy of the Incan shamans in which they also spoke of the time when the world turned upside down. He was fascinated to discover their strong belief that they'd come from the stars, calling themselves the children of the light.

Digging deeper, he discovered many stories of strange lights rising out from Lake Titikaka, located in Peru and Bolivia. The deep, mysterious lake has long been associated with extraterrestrial activity. He saw photographs of boulders that were cut in such a way that today's scientists and archeologists are baffled as to how a primitive race could cut with such precision using the technology of the time. He read about cities like Ollantaytambo in Peru in which parts of the city date back 12,000 years, and Teotihuacan in Mexico, whose three pyramids, like those in Egypt, align perfectly to the three stars in Orion's Belt in space.

How did his long-ago vision of the black triangles and the knowing of the world turning upside down tie into the strange encounters he was suddenly having?

The next logical step, as least in Alex's mind, was to research the subject of past lives. Already aware of his empathic abilities, he realized that, just as he could sense the energies of people around him, the past, present, and future are also energy. Time works as an energy. The analogy we gave at the beginning of this book serves as a perfect example. When we're in love or having a wonderful time, our vibration is high and time flies. When we're depressed or angry, our vibration is low and time drags.

As Alex analyzed each of the events when he'd transcended time, he became aware of a lightness of energy that would come over him. Then time, as he knew it, would disappear and he'd find himself in a different space – on the P-47 Thunderbolt, or in Ancient Rome. As an empath, he discovered there was no such thing as linear time. All the events he'd been through were there for him to experience when the access to that event was triggered, much like a song will trigger an emotional memory and bring the person right back to that place and time when they first heard the song.

He concluded that what was important wasn't time itself. It was the energy of the memory. In other words, standing in front of the P-47 Thunderbolt triggered the remembrance of his own death during World War II. Playing in the sandbox and looking up at the sky triggered the memory that those black triangles were coming back to get him as the world turned upside down.

Yet one question remained. How did this ability serve him personally? How did this help him in his daily life and on his spiritual journey? It was very disconcerting to be yanked out of the present and thrown back to a past life to experience events that were extremely painful emotionally. What was the point of it all?

Every event, memory, trauma, or situation we have ever lived through, whether in this life or another, is stored in our auric field and has a vibration to it. Part of that vibration is an emotional attachment to the moment or to a judgment of an experience. There was certainly an emotional attachment in Alex's experience of dying in the burning plane, or seeing his family ripped apart by lions in the Coliseum. When these experiences were triggered and came up again for Alex, he was able to re-experience them with what he had learned from being empathic. If he didn't label or judge something to be painful, draining, or anything within a fearful context, he was able to make different choices. His experience of the energy itself would change.

Rather than fear and hate the Romans for killing his family, he was able to forgive them. Rather than be burdened by guilt and despair at not doing enough to maneuver his P-47 Thunderbolt to safety, he was able to forgive himself, knowing he'd done the best he could. He was able to accept the circumstances from each of these situations and heal that part of himself that still clung to the anger or hurt. His new choices removed the fear and lightened him up emotionally, spiritually, and physically. It was as though a piece of his soul that had been unable to deal with the fear, the horror, the guilt, the anger, came back to him once he was able to heal and forgive. Not holding onto the lesser or heavier vibration of the past allowed him to see a more positive outcome in his future, which had not arrived yet. However, for that more positive outcome to arrive, he had to be present in the moment without emotional judgment of what he wanted it to be, nor allow the future to be clouded by the past.

Once he was able to piece all of this together, a sense of freedom made its way into Alex's life. His visions no longer tormented him. He no longer needed to change events that had happened in the past or continually relive them. In order to achieve this peace of mind, he needed to forgive, whether it was himself or others.

This is the ultimate healing tool. You simply need to be and experience events openly, without judgment, with the knowledge that everything is perfect. Even the most horrendous and painful events occur to serve as a lesson. It's part of your life plan. What needs to be learned will be learned.

Rather than use Alex, we'd like to use a personal story to illustrate the point of simultaneous time.

For years, Steve dreamt of Gettysburg, a town in southern Pennsylvania that was the site of one of the bloodiest, yet pivotal battles in America's Civil War. Over the course of three days in July 1863, over 50,000 men were killed, maimed, or reported missing in action. In each of his dreams, Steve witnessed himself marching in a line of men, wearing the blue uniform of a Union sergeant. He was weary, disgusted, and coping with an extreme aversion to being where he was, knowing instinctually that his life and the lives of his men were about to be wasted.

Ordered by his general to assemble in a place that made absolutely no sense militarily, since it left him and his men in too vulnerable a position, his frustration grew. Looking out over a large field, he saw that they were essentially sitting ducks. The Confederates had perfect aim to mow down his men in such an open position and it wasn't long before artillery fire and musket balls were decimating his unit. With a roar of fury at the incompetence of his general, and the needless waste of good, loyal men, he threw down his rifle and yelled out, "No more!"

At that moment, he felt a bullet tear into his back, after which he would awaken in a cold sweat. For that reason, he avoided any thoughts of going to Gettysburg.

Years later, he met Bety, who, as an historian, loved visiting historical locations. She cajoled and bullied until she finally convinced him to go to Gettysburg. During the eight-hour car ride, he considered turning back. His dream was so vivid, so heart-wrenching, he didn't think he had the courage to actually go to the place where it had happened. Yet, at the same time, he knew by going to Gettysburg, something significant would take place.

The February weather was cold and bleak, keeping the park empty of visitors by the time they arrived. Bundled up against the chilly winds, the small group walked along several fields, soaking in the energies that still linger from that fateful battle.

Strolling through one particular field, Steve suddenly came to an abrupt halt. The same emotions he'd experienced in the dream washed over him. He looked around him, sensing a deep familiarity with where he stood. He heard the sounds of his men, the explosion of cannon, the screams of the wounded. In that moment, Steve felt as though he was going to die. He wanted to run, but he couldn't. He was frozen to the spot in that cold, frost-covered field. He waited. He knew what was going to happen; he couldn't stop it. Bety came up to him, knowing Steve was in the middle of an intensely personal experience. She held space for him as he closed his eyes and shuddered. He heard himself declare, "No more!" He watched himself throw his rifle down. From behind him, he heard a yell, but he ignored it. Then he felt the agonizing pierce of a bullet rip into his back and he physically fell to the ground.

"Are you all right?" Bety exclaimed as she knelt down beside him.

Steve shook his head. "I've been shot."

They looked at each other in amazement. At that moment, he realized something powerful had happened here. The very fact that he was still here in physical form while reliving his death in another life validated the fact that we don't cease to exist once our body dies away. By remaining in the moment, in the present, he'd lived through the taking of his life. A calmness came over him.

At the same time, a member of the group, a man named David, burst into tears. It wasn't until he'd seen Steve "die" that he realized he too had been in that same battle. He'd watched his sergeant, his best friend, shot to death. He had a knowing that he'd survived the battle, come home from the war. But he'd been scarred by what he'd witnessed that day on the Gettysburg battlefield and it haunted him until that life came to an end.

Bety looked out over the open field, her face pensive. "I saw your death," she said quietly. "For some reason, I was able to tap into your vision. Do you know who shot you?"

Steve nodded. "My own captain," he said.

Bety agreed. "He was on a horse and came up riding behind you, yelling at you to pick up your rifle and charge the field. You refused. He then took out his revolver, calmly aimed at you, and shot you in the back."

David wiped his eyes. "That's exactly what I saw too."

"Do you know what this field is?" Bety asked. The men shook their heads.

Steve climbed to his feet. An energy pulled at him, drawing them towards the statue of a general. They walked over to it and Bety told them the story.

"This is General Sickles. He was told to form his troops over there," she said, pointing to the ridge behind her. "However, he disobeyed orders and formed his men here, in what's known as the Peach Orchard. It was a stupid move because it left his men open on three sides to attack by the Confederates. His superior officer was incensed, but it was too late to do anything. His troops were virtually all destroyed.

"It also makes perfect sense why your captain shot you. It was the sergeant's duty to shoot anyone who ran from a battle. By you refusing to fight, the captain had to ensure mass desertion didn't take place. He shot you as an example of what would happen to any man who tried to refuse to fight the way you did."

On that moment, Steve made a new energetic decision. Rather than believe he'd been a coward to throw his rifle down, he honored the decision he'd made on the battlefield that July 2, 1863. He'd known Sickles was wrong. He'd known a massacre was about to take place of the men he'd lived with, eaten with, cared about as though they were his brothers. He'd refused to take part in such a senseless act, sacrificing his life for doing so. In the magic of simultaneous time, he received that piece of his soul that had fled because he'd believed himself cowardly that day. He forgave himself, forgave the captain, forgave Sickles. He healed that moment in his own time line, and by so doing, helped David forgive and heal as well. He recognized what a wonderful opportunity both he and David had been given to heal. Grateful, they took it.

CHANGE ENERGY

As an empath, you are here to change energy. The first place this happens is with yourself. It is vital to try and emotionally heal your own traumas, whether from this life or previous lives. You may not actually see your past lives as Alex did, but you will carry a fear or an anger within you that was triggered by an event in the past – a fear of fire (did you die in a fire?), an unexplained pain in your neck (were you hung?), etc. You don't actually have to remember the event. Simply sit and feel the energy. Feel the fear of fire, or of heights, or whatever the fear is. Feel the anger, or the guilt or the sadness. Allow the energy to get stronger. Remember, it's all energy. It can't hurt you. Do not attach a story to the emotion. Simply feel it. You will find that as you feel the purity of the fear, or anger, or whatever the emotion is, it will begin to dissipate because there is no story for it to hold onto. If there is a memory attached to your emotion, go through the process of making different choices. Many times the choice is forgiveness, whether of another person or of yourself. Then remove the story and feel the purity of the emotion. Feel the anger, the fear, the guilt without the reason behind it. It will disappear and you will feel much lighter. It is as if the change to your past has now been relieved and released so that the Now is able to walk lighter into your future. In walking lighter into your future, you are not dragging the same lessons, or neediness or same undertakings of having to recreate reoccurring cyclical relationships, drama, traumas – all those things that are conceived by humans as outside themselves. As an empath knows, what you feel you become because of your ability to sense so deeply.

We know through our work that this process of experiencing and re-experiencing our past, present, and future is going to happen to each one of us at some point in our lives. There are many of you who may have found yourself in a certain place, experienced a certain trigger that brought an emotional awareness or discomfort to you. Try the exercise above and give yourself permission to forgive, to heal, to experience.

8

This Stuff Really Works

Manifesting, casting spells, throwing energy balls, projecting one's energy – it all works. However, they each have their own lessons and their own responsibilities. Then there's a little matter known as instant karma...

Alex needed a new car. Badly.

By this time, he'd done much work on himself: he'd started to heal his fears. He'd started to understand the mechanics of how energy works. He'd learned to ground and wasn't as affected as before by the dysfunctional energies around him. But one thing he did know: he definitely needed a car.

He searched the want ads, trying to get a feel for the type of car he wanted. An expensive car would be nice, yet, as an empath who already soaked up everyone's emotions, he knew he didn't want to attract that kind of attention to himself. He kept looking for the perfect vehicle, but nothing called out to him, so he let it go.

That night, while lying in bed, thoughts of a car popped into his head again. Alex said a little prayer, asking that his guidance provide him with a clue, a message, anything that could help him find the car that was right for him. He closed his eyes and promptly fell asleep.

It wasn't long before he saw himself winding down bumpy, country roads. Looking about him, he saw he was in a green-colored jeep.

The dream continued. Certain details became clear. One of the bigger details was the number "13" flashing before his eyes. When he awoke, he knew he had to find this jeep. But where was it? How in heaven's name was he ever going to find it? The dream neglected to tell him that. He nevertheless checked how much money he had. To his amusement, he saw he had exactly $1,300 with which to pay for this jeep.

He put the money on the kitchen table and declared to his family, "I have $1,300 and today I will find a jeep."

Having dealt with Alex's dramatic statements for many years, his family nodded politely, then ignored him completely.

He borrowed the family car and drove along local roads. As he did so, he paid close attention to the energy around him. He physically felt the pull of the desire for this jeep. Before he knew what he was doing, he started to follow the energy – turning down roads where the pull was strongest to turning around when the pull felt weak or non-existent. Although he didn't know enough at the time to put a name to what he was doing, he was in essence tracking the energy – following the pull of an invisible thread to its inevitable destination.

Suddenly, he saw a dirt road loom up ahead of him. It looked very familiar. The energy pull was the strongest it had been all day. Could this be the same dirt road he saw himself driving down in his dream? Only one way to find out.

At the end of the long bumpy road, deep in the woods, he found himself in the front yard of an old ramshackle house. There, parked in front of a precariously leaning garage was the green jeep, with a "For Sale" sign on it. The vehicle wasn't pretty, but this had to be the jeep he'd dreamt about. He went to the door, knocked, and an older gentleman came out.

"I'm interested in buying that jeep over there," Alex told him.

"It's not much," the old man admitted. "It's been driven hard. But it's time for me to let it go." He looked Alex up and down. "Price is firm," he said.

"How much?"

"$1,300. Not a penny less."

Alex sensed the old man hold his breath as if ready for a fight over the price of the jeep. However, excited that he'd actually found the vehicle he knew was meant for him, validated more now by the fact that the price was exactly how much Alex had in his pocket, he handed over the cash.

After getting the bill of sale and telling the old man he'd be back later that day to pick up the jeep, he drove away. His energy was high; he was pumped up as he marveled over the magic of manifestation. He was grateful to see how he could use his empathic ability for something stronger than just keeping heavy emotions away. So this is part of what it means to be an empath, he thought to himself as he drove home. Thank you!

Arriving home, he told his family about his good fortune. His younger brother, curious to see this gifted jeep Alex was jabbering on about, offered to give him a ride back to pick up the vehicle.

When they arrived at the old man's house, Alex eagerly jumped into the jeep and turned the key. The only sound he heard was his brother's snickering. He tried again. Nothing.

"I can get that started for you," the old man said as he appeared at the driver's side window. "We'll give it a jump."

He opened the hood and ambled off to get a pair of jumper cables. Alex got out of the jeep and took a look under the hood. His heart sank.

The belts were worn, there were oil leaks everywhere. Once again he heard his brother laughing behind him.

"Great gift, Alex!" he heckled. "The only gift is going to be if that piece of crap actually runs."

Alex began to doubt the wisdom of his purchase. He'd been so caught up in the energy, maybe he should have looked a little more fully at this jeep.

No! he thought emphatically to himself. The energy wouldn't lie to me. I'm supposed to have this jeep.

As promised, the old man was able to get the jeep started. Following his brother down the bumpy dirt road, Alex began to regain confidence in his purchase. The jeep was handling the bumps superbly.

When they pulled out onto the main road, Alex's brother accelerated and Alex followed suit. To his dismay, the jeep began to rattle. The more he accelerated, the more the jeep rattled as if it were ready to fall apart. He had no choice but to slow down and watch his brother disappear down the road. Once again, he was overcome with fear that he'd made a terrible mistake. His energy fell.

When he finally arrived home, he crawled under the jeep to take a look. Fear grew into despair. His golden purchase, his desired manifestation, that gift in the dream, now looked more like a curse.

Yet once again, Alex knew deep down inside that for whatever reason, he was meant to have this jeep. He pushed aside the despair. He was a good mechanic. He could make this work.

He took a week off from work and began to diligently fix up the jeep, replacing lights, oil, plugs. He spent hours scrapping the rust from the frame. In the midst of all this, he decided that with a bit of ingenuity, he could make this jeep unique to himself.

Going to the local hardware store, he found the perfect color that would spruce up the jeep. It was a textured spray paint called granite that reminded him of the stones he loved so deeply.

After all the hard work, the day came when Alex was done. He took a step back and looked at the newly painted jeep. A deep sense of accomplishment filled him. There had been a purpose to the manifestation of the jeep. Despite those moments when he'd doubted because the jeep wasn't living up to his own preconceived expectations of what it should be, he'd held fast. In so doing, he learned the lesson of trusting because, in the end, the jeep ended up being exactly what he needed and wanted.

About a year later, Alex's band was playing at a house located deep in the woods. As he'd done many times, he used his jeep to transport his music equipment, parking it close to the stage to unload the amps. In a break between sets, he noticed a pair of older gentlemen inspecting his jeep. The resemblance between the two told him they were brothers. They were deep in thought, pointing at the jeep and whispering between themselves.

Hesitantly, Alex approached them.

"Can I help you?" he asked.

One of the men, reminiscent of the old man who'd sold him the jeep, replied, "You own this?"

Alex nodded. "For about a year. Why?"

One of the men shook his head. "I think this was ours once upon a time. We sold it about ten years ago to an old man. Hate to admit it, but we thought we'd gotten one over on him. This piece of crap was never going to run again. But look at it. You've made it so beautiful. It's a real keeper now."

Alex's heart opened. "With a little trust and hard work, you'd be surprised at what you can create when you see something as a negative and turn it into a positive."

One of the most profound talents an empath possesses is the ability to track energy. Every thought, every feeling leaves a physical presence that makes its way to the object of the thought. In other words, if you think about an apple, the energy of that thought makes its way to an apple. You have now anchored your thought and emotions to an object (the apple).

The more work you do on yourself, the more healing that takes place, the easier it is for the physical act of manifestation to take place. As with Alex and his jeep, he'd done a great deal of self-healing, leaving him open to guidance, especially in the dreamtime. By paying attention and trusting, he was able to track the energy and find his jeep. At first glance, the jeep wasn't anything special. In fact, it was a piece of junk. Yet Alex believed in his vision, believed in the energy he'd been following. More importantly, he believed in the guidance he'd been given in the dreamtime. He took something that appeared to be negative and made it into a positive. His jeep now became the envy of others.

By paying attention, great things can unfold in the world of manifestation.

However, a great deal of self-healing needs to take place because, as a rule, most humans manifest from a place of fear.

Look around you. How many people do you know who are truly satisfied with what they have? Do they believe they have enough? Do they want to be more attractive? Garner more attention? Have more money?

Many project the energy of neediness. If I get this, I'll be happy. If I get that, I'll feel better about myself. I need these things to be fulfilled.

Their desires and their neediness attach to their energies and it is these energies that go out and attempts to draw to them those things they think they need to fulfill those empty spaces of energy within them.

Some people believe if they have the perfect job, the perfect mate, a beautiful home, the newest electronic device, all their wants and desires will be fulfilled and they won't need to be validated anymore. What they don't understand is that these material things are false validations. As we've said before, untrue energy doesn't last. It's fleeting. As soon as they draw what they think they need to themselves, the feeling of fulfillment lasts only a little while, before they once again feel the need to draw more to themselves to fill up the empty spaces within them. They look outside themselves for validation through the use of material objects.

Love itself is a validation. People seek love outside themselves, rather than understand that love starts within. You must love yourself first before you can love someone else. And if you are okay with yourself, comfortable in your own skin, you don't need the validation of someone else to make you whole.

Empaths learn this earlier than most people.

As you endeavor to draw to yourself love and the belief that you're not different, you have to face the thought that you're doing this in order to feel validated. Most people do.

This is the state our world is in. And this is the lesson for the empath.

Alex needed a jeep. This is a basic need for anyone who lives outside a city where public transportation is not accessible. We need to get to work. We need to buy groceries. The only way to accomplish this is through the use of a car. Now Alex could have picked a Cadillac or a fancy sports car. Yet his dream presented him with an opportunity to own something that would best serve him beyond his own needs or desires. A lesson was presented that would teach him something bigger than just buying him something to get him to work.

As he drew the energy of the jeep to himself, he realized he could be directed. There was a path for him to follow, there was guidance looking out for him. He had to look past his natural distrust of people and have the courage to deal with the old man. Even in his momentary despair that he'd made a terrible mistake buying the jeep, he still followed through. By trusting that the jeep was gifted to him by his guidance, the jeep turned into a wonderful thing in his life. He could take this jeep into his beloved woods. He loved tinkering with it, making it his. When the two gentlemen at the party told him they thought this jeep would never drive again, he loved the satisfaction that he'd made it drivable. He'd held the space of the energy and trusted and been gifted with exactly what he needed.

There was another side to this lesson for Alex to learn, however. This had to do with money.

In a dream, Alex saw himself holding a lot of money. As he held the money, he sensed a great deal of attention focused on him; people wanting to possess him, more material objects coming his way. During his waking hours, he began to think about the money. What would it be like to have this much money? He wouldn't need to worry anymore about being unable to buy those things he liked. He could move to a bigger place, buy nicer clothes. People would look at him differently. Treat him better. Maybe he could actually use this money to make a difference in people's lives.

The money dreams continued. His hopes grew. How nice it would be not having to work anymore. How wonderful it would be to buy bigger, better things.

Caught up as he was in the fantasy of being rich, he missed the lesson that was being presented. Like everything else, money has its own vibrational energy. However, blinded by the idea of wealth, Alex wasn't sensing the energy. One night he saw a scratch ticket in his dreams. It had the winning amount of $400,000. This was surely enough to change his life.

That night, while driving to a friend's house, Alex suddenly saw a vision of dollar signs flashing before his eyes. It almost blinded him as he held onto his steering wheel.

"Oh my God!" he instantly thought. "It's time! I'm going to win $400,000."

He started to pay attention. He started to track the energy as he'd done with the jeep. In the middle of this, he found himself overcome with an inexplicable fear that someone else would buy his lottery ticket. Someone else would win his money.

He drove faster. Coming to an intersection he saw in front of him a gas station with a quickie mart. He knew this gas station. He'd stopped here many times on his way to work to buy a coffee. He knew they sold scratch tickets there. He was filled with an irrational impatience. He had to get in there before someone else bought his ticket. He became frantic. In his frenzy, he started to go through the stop sign. Suddenly, he heard a voice yell in his ear, "Pay attention!"

He slammed on his brakes. At that moment, a speeding tractor truck flew by, missing him by inches.

Alex sat there in shock. What the hell had just happened?

He slowly pulled into the quickie mart's parking lot and turned off the jeep. Shaking badly, he tried his best to calm down. He realized in that moment that the dollar signs flashing in his mind's eye were gone. He no longer felt the frenzied need to buy the lottery ticket. The energy that had been pushing him forward was no longer there. All he could think about was how close he'd come to being killed. If he hadn't heard his guidance yell at him to pay attention, he would no longer be alive. Slowly, his energy settled down and a sense of calm swept over him.

He began to analyze what had just happened.

Rather than accept the possibility that money might be coming to him and leave it at that, he'd attached all sorts of energy to his dream. He'd created an untruth to the energy of the money. Could it be that he'd become so caught up in the energy of greed that it had almost cost him his life?

True manifestation happens when it's supposed to happen. All things that are given, all things that are truly manifested from a place of service, either for yourself or others, are tools, opportunities, and options to teach. He realized what he'd just been through was a huge lesson. He'd been blinded by something he didn't truly need in his life. He had what he needed. Perhaps if he had the large house, the bigger cars, the nicer clothes, his path would change and the opportunities to learn what it means to be an empath would not be learned. Other things would captivate his attention, things he didn't truly need to make him happy.

Rather than the good energy he'd felt when he'd found his jeep, he now felt the heavier energy of greed. Deciding not to buy the scratch ticket, he drove off, knowing that what he needed would be presented to him as he grew into his knowledge of empathy.

Driving along, he looked back at other times in his life where he'd abused his newfound ability to manifest.

In the Asian energy traditions, there are balls of energy called Chi balls. By rubbing your hands together vigorously, then holding your palms about five inches apart, you can actually feel a ball of energy between your hands.

Alex remembered an evening when he'd gone club-hopping with a group of friends. Standing at the bar, he noticed an attractive young lady across the room.

"Look at this," he told his friends. "I'm going to get her attention."

He rubbed his hands together and watched the energy grow. By this time, he knew that colors of energy elicited different responses from people. He made his energy ball a vibrant red, the color of passion. Of lust. He knew his friends couldn't see what he was doing, but he was eager to show off. He threw the ball at the girl. She instantly looked around. Alex laughed while his friends stood in awe. He did it again. Once again, she turned around to see who had touched her. This time, however, her face was contorted in anger. In that moment, Alex felt her anger. A doorway opened. Now instead of feeling just her emotional turmoil, he physically felt the emotions of everyone in the club – their needs, wants, lusts, desires. He became overwhelmed with heaviness. His muscles and head began to ache; his heart clenched. He was finding it hard to breathe.

"I've got to go," he told his friends as he turned and hurried out of the club.

Sitting in his car, he tried to figure out what had happened. He was just having fun, playing around with these newfound abilities. How had that triggered the awful way he was feeling right now?

The answer slowly came to him.

Instant Karma.

More than just the title of a John Lennon song, he'd read about instant Karma in his religious studies. The theory was that when you did something negative, a retribution would find its way to you. There was also the Law of Three. Whatever you put out comes back to you threefold.

Could it really be that instant? Had what he'd done in the club, however innocent, now rebounded on him so quickly?

He went home and cleared himself as best he could. That night he had a dream.

He dreamt he was in a helicopter with a Green Beret soldier pilot. They spent the night flying through the jungle, enjoying each other's company. The soldier laughed and smiled, and Alex thoroughly enjoyed himself. When the helicopter landed, Alex asked the soldier who he was.

"I've killed people," he answered. "I have to stay here."

A look of despair replaced the look of joy he'd had just moments earlier. Alex immediately felt the soldier's energy. It was the same energy he'd experienced in the club. The heaviness of guilt and anger. He once again asked the soldier who he was. He received the same answer. "I've killed people. I have to stay here."

Then Alex awoke.

Thinking it over, Alex realized that because he was empathic, his learning and understanding of energy was different from those who weren't as empathic. As he gave, so he received. As he received, so he gave.

In the moment that he gave from a place of need and want – wanting the girl's attention in the club, needing his friends' approval – he drew all the energy of the club to himself. Choosing to use his gifts in a negative way, using something so divine to be used as his version of love to attract attention got him what he wanted – the energetic attention of everyone in the club, with all the emotional baggage attached to that energy.

He also contemplated the words of the helicopter pilot. What did he mean when he told Alex he'd killed, so he had to stay where he was? Was there some kind of instant Karma to that as well?

Was part of instant Karma the inability to leave the energy you've labeled? The pilot had labeled his energy as guilt. Even though he was performing his duty as a soldier protecting his country, he'd labeled his energy with that of guilt – a lower vibrational energy. By doing that, he was now stuck in some kind of karmic merry-go-round.

Later that morning, Alex called his friends.

"Hey dude, you missed a great night last night! We had a great time. Met some very foxy ladies. What the hell happened to you?"

As he listened to their words, his energy sank. He felt awful for missing out on such an enjoyable evening. As the heaviness descended over him, he couldn't ground it out fast enough. It was now becoming part of who he was at that moment. He sighed.

"I didn't feel well. I did something I shouldn't have done last night. I'm very sorry about that."

The energy abruptly changed. The heaviness lifted off. He was amazed. Was it that simple? By admitting to the truth of what he'd done and truly feeling remorseful, was it possible for the energy of instant Karma to be moved?

He hung up and contemplated what he'd just learned.

INTENTION

Pay attention to your intentions. What is really needed in your life and why? This will begin to show you what your path truly is. Many times our intentions or needs are coming from a place of neediness of what we've been taught we need. Magazines and television scream at us to wear the latest fashion, eat the trendiest foods, possess the newest toys. Most of the time, our neediness comes from a place of fear. From a place of preconceived lack. It seems that in this fast-paced world, what we have is never enough. We are judged by what we own. And condemned for what we don't own. This need becomes, in its own way, a merry-go-round of needing and wanting more and more to fulfill us. It's all false. If something comes up that you feel you must have, take a moment and look at it. Do you really need it? Will it really make a difference in your life? Will what you need propel you forward into attaining a higher truth, or will it fade away and create another vacuum that will need to be filled again once the novelty wears off? Look at the emotions behind the need. The emotion of greed almost got Alex killed. The emotion of getting the girl's attention by misusing his gifts caused Alex physical pain. Did he really need those things? No. But they served as a wonderful tool to teach.

As an empath, you will be presented with multiple opportunities to learn. Take them and allow them to lead you to a higher truth, to an understanding of what it means to be an empath. Start to look at the energies and ask yourself, do I need this to validate some need within myself? Do I need that person's love to validate me as a human being? Do I need the newest car, the latest fashion to show off to my friends? No matter what happens in your life, see the events as a learning tool. Only by experiencing do we learn. Remember: you are here to change energy for the better. Allow yourself to be led towards that goal.

9

Manifestation 101

An empath's guide to manifesting responsibly.

One of the most prevalent subjects you'll find in any new-age section of a bookstore has to do with the art of manifestation. Do you want more money? Manifest it. Do you want the love of your life to show up? Do you want a mansion, or a Mercedes, or the newest electronic gadget? Manifest it.

All these books and articles and CDs make it sound so easy. Naturally, Alex read these books, listened to the CDs. He too wanted all the things he was promised he could manifest. He tried the positive thinking; he filled notebooks with positive affirmations. By now he knew everything had an energy to it. That energy could either empower or disempower him. Still, there was a pull to these items, just as there had been a pull for him to purchase the jeep. Look how wonderful that had turned out to be.

One day his friends asked him to accompany them on a week-long hike along the Appalachian Trail. Alex jumped at the chance. He loved the woods and could think of nothing better than spending a week among the trees and mountains. Nature was his element and he liked the idea of showing his true self to his friends in a place that made him feel safe.

He took out his hiking equipment and his stomach fell. This was a much longer hike than he was used to. He could probably get by with the sleeping bag, but the rain pants were definitely going to have to be replaced.

As he rolled up the sleeping bag, a part of him longed to have a nicer one. He wanted to show off to his friends what a proficient outdoorsman he truly was. How could he do that with such a ratty sleeping bag? They'd laugh at his pathetic equipment. Unfortunately, a good sleeping bag cost money that he didn't have.

Nevertheless, he looked through all the camping magazines. He sighed at the beautiful equipment and groaned at the ridiculously high prices. Still, he had a month before the trip. If he could manifest a jeep, he could manifest the hiking gear. So he did what he'd done before. He put it out to the universe that needed rain pants and a sleeping bag, then put it out of his mind.

A few days later he was in the cafeteria at work when he saw a pile of sales flyers on the counter. Picking it up, he was astonished to see that the local sporting goods store was having a sale. He was further astonished to see that the rain pants he needed were on sale! What luck! The sale price was exactly what he could afford.

Alex puffed up with self-satisfaction. The manifesting process was working. He really was a pretty powerful guy to make this happen.

After getting paid, Alex made his way down to the sporting goods store. Heading straight for the clothing department, he found the rain pants. They were the last pair and they were in his size. God, what a great manifestor he was!

On his way to the register, he felt a pull towards the sleeping bags. He hesitated. He had just enough money for the rain pants. He should just buy them and leave. However, he thought about how he'd look in front of his friends with his sleek, new, state-of-the-art sleeping bag. It wouldn't hurt to just take a look at them, would it?

Sure enough, when he entered the department, there it was, the same model he'd drooled over in the camping magazines. He shook it out, enjoying the feel of the material and how light and sleek it was. He saw himself sleeping in this bag, enjoying the envious looks of his friends when they saw he had the latest in sleeping equipment. Suddenly it became important to him to look good in front of his friends. He felt a heaviness of energy, but pushed it away at the thought of preening and showing off in front of his buddies. At that moment, a salesperson came up.

"Can I help you with anything?" the man asked.

"I'm going on a week-long hike," Alex explained. "Just getting some ideas on what to take with me."

The man smiled. "You couldn't have picked a better sleeping bag. It's highly durable, great in all kinds of weather. And it just happens to be on sale, today only. This year's models are coming out next week; we have to make room for the newer inventory."

"Really? How much for this bag?"

When the salesperson gave him the price, Alex's jaw dropped. It was more than half off the regular price. Could this be? Alex asked him to repeat the price. Once more the salesperson repeated the outrageously low price. Alex's energy increased. Damn, he'd done it again! He'd manifested exactly what he wanted. He looked down at the rain pants. He couldn't afford both, but he was willing to sacrifice the pants for the sleeping bag. With thoughts on how cool he was going to look in front of his friends, he put the rain pants back.

"If the register gives you any problems, call me," the salesperson replied.

Alex nodded and practically ran to the register with his fantastic purchase.

The cashier rang it up. When Alex saw the price, a fear washed over him. It was the full price.

"I was told this was on sale for $49.95," he replied.

"That can't be true. This retails for $250.00," she answered.

"I was told by the salesperson it was $49.95," Alex remarked.

She pursed her lips. "I'll have to check with the manager."

While she paged the manager, a line formed behind Alex. He felt their annoyance, their impatience. Their energy began to fill him up.

The manager arrived and the cashier explained the situation.

"Who told you this sleeping bag was $49.95?" the manager demanded.

Alex's energy took a nose-dive. He didn't want to get the salesperson in trouble, but he really wanted the sleeping bag. He told the manager the salesperson's name. A moment later he was paged and arrived at the register.

"Did you tell this customer the price of the bag was $49.95?"

Now Alex felt the anger of the manager and the fear of the salesperson.

"Maybe I made a mistake," the salesperson admitted meekly.

Negativity consumed Alex. Was he somehow taking advantage of the store? Was this salesperson going to be fired because of him?

The manager turned to Alex. "I can't give you the bag for $49.95. But what I'll do is give you a 20% discount."

"Do you take layaway?" Alex asked.

"No. But I will hold it for you until tomorrow."

Alex thanked the manager, then made his way back to at least buy the rain pants. To his dismay, they were gone.

Walking back to his car, he knew the whole day had been a complete wash. He couldn't afford the sleeping bag, yet the purchase of the rain pants hadn't been allowed either.

In his mind's eye, he saw the manager of the store, sitting behind his desk, counting his profits as the items in his store, including the sleeping bag and rain pants, were purchased. Alex's energy grew heavy as it aligned with the energy of the money. He then recalled the annoyance of the people in line behind him, the irritation of the cashier, the fear of the salesperson. All that energy also felt heavy. He was reminded once more of the apple. When the apple was allowed to connect to earth and gather light, it became perfect. It became what the apple should be. When the apple became filled with the energy of money and profits and others' intentions, it wasn't perfect anymore.

Alex realized he'd done the same thing with the sleeping bag. He didn't really need it. He'd only wanted it to look good in front of his friends. The whole thing had blown up in his face because he'd been trying to force something that he didn't really need. The rain pants, however, felt good when he'd held them in his hands. Yet what had he done? He'd removed the one thing that truly was a gift and gone for what he thought was a bigger gift, only to have it all go wrong. He'd gotten in the way of the gift of the rain pants and ruined it. His energy plummeted and as he sat in his car, he felt drained and tired.

Was it possible that if he aligned to those things that didn't serve him, or tried to manifest things that weren't part of what he really needed, the heaviness of their energy would find their way to him? When he'd held the rain gear, he felt fine, as if this was supposed to happen, as it had with his jeep. When he shifted into trying to force a manifestation to happen with the sleeping bag, it made him feel heavy and drained.

Hopefully you've begun to understand that as an empath, you are different from other people. You are a human sponge and nothing is going to change that. You've realized that everything that happens, everything that we feel is energy. Good energy, bad energy...it's all just energy.

You've also begun to see how people use their energy as a tool or a weapon. They try to get a reaction from you. You give it to them. By reacting, you leak your energy to them. They walk away feeling energized because you've allowed them to take your energy, while you're exhausted because you allowed them to take your energy.

No one can take your energy unless you allow it.

On the foundation you're building of what it means to be an empath, you will have learned, or at least felt, when words people use don't always match their intentions. You will have tried to protect yourself against all of this by putting up walls, by retreating from the world, by using protection to ward it all away, only to realize that you've only managed to either attract more to yourself or turned yourself into someone you don't even know. As you experience and learn from all of these situations, you will begin to understand that what you've been going through is a type of spiritual boot camp. Only by getting through spiritual boot camp are you going to learn what being an empath is all about. You've learned that you can't hide forever from feeling. You've learned that whenever you react, you're adding more gunk to the growing pile of human-induced emotional gunk. Through grounding and transparency, you've learned that you're here to move and change the vibration of all the energy you're feeling. And as you've gotten through your trials and seen them for what they are, you've begun to understand there truly is a method behind the madness of how the world energetically works and what your role in it is.

Manifestation is part of this. As your vibration goes up, it allows you to more fully tap into physical manifestation because, as with everything else, there is a vibration to the manifestation. Match up those vibrations and you will find yourself manifesting things.

However, what is not mentioned in many of these manifestation books and manuals is the responsibility of manifesting. The foundation of manifestation is the emotion known as desire. Who hasn't felt desire, whether for a person or an object? There's a pull to it. It can become very addicting, because it's a human pull to fulfill something you need (or think you need).

Empaths have the opportunity to learn how energy feels and how it aligns. When it aligns in your life and you are brought what you need; the energy feels good. There is an energetic context that fits into the overall plan of your life. It is as if all cylinders are working in unison. When something is manifested to fit into your life plan, there is minimal effort needed. Pieces fall into place, seemingly effortlessly. The energy flows unimpeded. You don't have to work so hard at it.

We all have a destiny. And, as with everything else, your destiny has an energetic vibration to it. Things are brought to you to test and learn about this energy. The basics of your existence has energy and the empath becomes sensitive to it – whether it's food that no longer resonates with you, thought processes, or religious and political beliefs that don't fit into the scheme of your life. As an empath, you have choices. You have the option to learn, or the option to hide; the choice to accept all as a lesson and the choice to label everything as negative. This is a golden opportunity to learn what is true and what isn't.

It's also an opportunity to learn how empaths can use their energy for change. It doesn't take much to see how people latch onto things and situations, putting all their being into believing it will bring them fame, fortune, validation, feeling despair if they lose it all. As an empath, you know that the energies of life aren't draining. You don't need to be overwhelmed if you lose something materially. The essence of our life is to experience. To be in the flow of the pure energy. In that flow, things are perfect. If you align your energies, your money, your time into any given situation, what you need will be brought to you. You will be provided the tools to further your existence. You will be provided those situations that will teach you bigger and better lessons.

We don't believe money or big houses or electronic toys are bad. They have their own energies to them. They all come from Source and have a connection to the earth. They all have their job to do. It is when we put untruths into this energy that the works get gummed up. If that energy is not in alignment to your destiny, the energy feels lousy.

How many similar relationships do we need to go through before we realize we don't need to keep being the victim, keep bargaining ourselves away, keep trying to change the other person? How many times do we need to keep being dishonored in order to fit in? How many drinks, or drugs, or cigarettes do we need to attain that false grounding; that false good feeling that always fades when the drinks or drugs or nicotine wear off?

Sensing this and aligning with a higher energy is part of your energetic destiny. This is your knowing as an empath. This is how true manifestation works.

When you manifest from a place of your own will, you must expend more of your energy to keep the manifestation going. It becomes exhausting because you're not aligning to the energy of Source to manifest. You're using up all of your own energy to make something happen. Why is this? Because when you go into a place of desire or want from your own place of ego, there's actually a disconnect from Source energy. The second you take yourself out of truth – out of your destiny – the energy from Source shuts off. It does this because Source won't pour more energy into a dysfunctional situation and amplify it. When that happens, you have no choice but to project your own energy, draining yourself and lowering your vibration. The manifestation wanes because it's not being created for your best interests.

However, if you are aligned to Source, aligned to what your path is, and if part of your path is having the newest electronic toy or newest car, you find you don't need to work very hard for it. It appears. And you don't need to "keep it going." It happens automatically. Those things that are in your best interest manifest without much work on your part.

The responsibility of manifesting lies in the type of energy you're putting out there. Remember, as an empath who has done the work, your vibration is already pretty high. That high energy is what you're putting out there. If you're aligned to Source and you're needed to be at a particular place at a particular time because that space or person may need your higher vibration, whatever you need to get to that place will be manifested. We can attest to the truth of this because it has happened many times in our own lives. However, if you align to your own will and are manifesting those things that don't serve you, you're now putting out energy that is vibrating at a much lower frequency. Instead of helping clean up the energetic mess, you're adding to it.

TRUST

There's a huge measure of trust to this. However, after going through these situations ourselves, we've learned to trust that we will be taken care of. We've consciously aligned our will to a higher will and find that what we need comes to us without a lot of effort on our part.

In 2012, an opportunity arose for Steve, Bety, and a group of their friends to travel to Peru. Bety wasn't sure she'd be able to go. There were bills to pay and she didn't know where she could come up with the money necessary for the trip. One night, she prayed to her guidance and told them, "If you need me to go on this trip, you'll have to find a way to help me find the money, because I sure can't figure out where to get it." She then stopped thinking about it and went on with her life. About two weeks later, her boss called her into his office and informed her that one of her co-workers had to take an unexpected leave of absence. Would she be willing to work extra days to keep up with the workload? Bety smiled. Of course she wouldn't mind! Without any effort on her part, the Universe had provided a way for her to earn the money to go to Peru.

It's important not to put energy into the outcome of any situation. Let the Universe work without human intention. If it's meant to happen, it will, just as it did for Bety. Trust that what you need will be brought to you.

10

It's All a Test

Many times you will experience things that test your fears: a vision, a dream, a particularly unnerving situation. It is all part of learning how you and others use their energy. As you learn to overcome your fears, more psychic gifts and abilities are given that allows you to more fully step onto your path.

Whether you're empathic or not, the world we live in tests us every day. However, being an empath sometimes makes us feel that the tests are way over the top because many times you're not only feeling what you're going through, but you're also feeling what others around you are going through. This is why many empaths consider their gift of empathy a curse.

There are four energetic bodies that an empath, by virtue of being an empath, is tied into more so than the average person. These are the emotional, mental, physical, and spiritual bodies. Each one of these bodies offers their own set of lessons. But they also offer the empath unique gifts.

The emotional body gives you the ability to sense, understand, and read, not only your energy, but also others' energy, including that of animals and nature. You get a sense of where they've been, what they're feeling and why. But what if the emotional energy has become so uncomfortable it becomes the enemy – something to be avoided at all costs? What if it drives you to experience only what you perceive to be "good" emotion? In this sense, oftentimes you will feel as though there's a wolf nipping at your heels to keep you away from all those experiences you feel are not good for you. When this happens, you've set up a duality in your emotional body. It now becomes a battle of you versus your emotions. All those fears, all those thoughts of what you deem as bad are now part of your emotional body, lowering your vibration and exhausting you. That lower vibration prevents you from just being open and present and allowing whatever energy is around you to simply flow. Those lower vibrations are shutting you down like a faucet. You no longer allow the energy to flow out your feet because you've turned yourself off.

The mental body helps you understand how powerful your thoughts are. It is this body that puts your thoughts into physical manifestation. It is also the mental body that allows you to transcend astral planes when you meditate by setting forth the intention of what you hope to achieve. However, this is also the problem of the mental body. The mental body is only as strong as what it has experienced. Everything that happens in your life is presented as an opportunity to experience energy. If that energy in the moment is looked upon as a negative, the mental body makes a catalogue of negative energies of the experiences. Therefore, the mental body can only work from its past and what it has learned. Now you've set up a duality in the mental body. If you think you know more, then you think you'll be safe. However, there's a problem in that – the problem of knowing and not knowing. Or rather what you think you know as opposed to what is really there.

Knowledge can be perceived in an instant by the energy that's presented. When a situation occurs, you pull from your own past catalogue of knowledge. When you do that, you are bringing forth a judgment or a declaration that this moment, this situation means whatever I've experienced in the past. Energy, however, doesn't work this way. Energy just wants to be experienced. By allowing yourself to simply experience the energy, a new knowledge can present itself. For example, you see a dog. Your perception may be different from another person who sees the same dog. You love dogs because you grew up with dogs. You feel happy to see the dog. The other person, however, may have been attacked by a dog when they were younger. Each of you will put out a different energy from whatever mental file you both have pulled from the catalogue in your mind. In that instant, the two of you have added your own self-energy into the experience and the opportunity is lost to truly understand what the experience was truly about. You can see this when an empath comes into a new experience.

If you were to walk into a room filled with fifteen people, each from a different country, with different clothing, different languages, different physical appearances, the choice for you as an empath is to remain open and experience whatever is there to experience. However, if you walk into that room and allow the duality of the past to already make a judgment of something you think you know, either because of what you've seen on television, or been taught by your parents or peers, this does not serve the energy. Energy is only served when you're open to experience what needs to be experienced. When that is allowed to occur, you now add something new to your mental catalogue.

The physical body is the manifestation of self here on the earth plane. It is the repository of your soul. The physical body is what allows you to begin the learning process of how energy works and how it affects you because you physically feel it – whether it's phantom pain or heartache, or in some cases, a physical discomfort when you come in contact with a lower energy.

Here is another learning that is necessary in your journey as an empath. Because you so strongly feel your surroundings, that feeling can root itself in the physical body and become something that you try to overcome. If it doesn't feel good, you react and try to move it away from the physical body. You go back into your mental catalogue and pull out the file card that says, I went through this before and it wasn't good. You put that judgment into the energy you're feeling. However, it actually serves you better from a higher perspective if you can move the energy out of your physical body and not react to the physical pains.

Many empaths become, through no fault of their own, hypochondriacs because they haven't learned boundaries – where they end and another begins. Because you feel everybody's emotions, their pain becomes your pain. If you start to go into the mental body thought process of what's wrong with me, why do I feel so deeply, why does it always physically hurt, you begin to accumulate these energies within your body. That's when panic and anxiety attacks occur. This energy needs to go somewhere. If you allow the energy to flow through and complete its route by grounding and not reacting to it, the physical pain goes away. It dissipates because it has nothing to hold onto anymore and will flow out of you. This is how you will be able to differentiate between phantom pain and real physical pain. If you witness the pain by not labeling it or attaching a story to it and it dissipates, you know it's an energy. However, if you do these steps and the pain does not go away, you know it's your body telling you something is wrong. Take whatever action is necessary, including medical treatment. As an empath, you've probably spent your life policing your body. You have a better sense of what you're going through physically.

The spiritual body is the aura that surrounds every living creature, including trees and rocks. It is in the spiritual body where your past, present, and future resides. Those who can see and read auras can tell you where traumas have taken place in any one of your lifetimes. It can also give you warnings of health issues that may be coming up. Through the unfoldment of the lessons of the spiritual body, opportunities of life present themselves. The energy of the spiritual body creates everyday realities, chances to bring you into a truer sense of being. However, as in the other bodies, you can also get stuck in thoughts of duality – good and evil, black and white. The gifts of divination, healing, mediumship, and more come from your ability to sense and understand and read energy in those around you. You are able to tap into the universal energy that is all around us and see what has happened and, many times, what will happen. This is where the four bodies start to truly work together. The higher energy of each of the four bodies come together and teaches you what it means to be an empath. Here is where you begin to learn to take away labels of what the emotional body is feeling. The same is true for the mental and physical bodies. By not allowing the old thoughts and beliefs to take root, the energy has nothing to grasp onto. It dissipates and moves through you quickly. If the pain you're feeling is an energetic pain, either from coming in contact with someone with lower vibrational energy, or from a judgment you've made, if you see it as an opportunity to witness and let go, the pain will leave.

To get to this point, you will have had to go through spiritual boot camp as described in prior chapters. But if you've done the work, these four bodies can be brought to a place of higher knowing. How?

By becoming transparent. By removing as many of your own blocks (or fears) as you can. Keep in mind the analogy of the beaver building his dam. Anything behind the dam is going to get clogged up and stuck. However, when the dam is removed, the energy flows freely through you, doing what it's supposed to do – keeping you connected to a higher source of pure energy. Your connection to Source is what will allow you to stay balanced, to function at a higher vibrational level – to see, hear, and feel more clearly because there isn't any "gunk" getting in your way.

As we've stated throughout this book, an empath's job is to offset the negativity of the world. It's the same thing with thoughts and feelings, whether emotional or physical or even spiritual. As those thoughts and feelings that are not rooted in truth get moved out of the way, the energy flows more freely. You begin to connect to the pure source of energy that feels like a love you've never experienced on the earth plane.

More spiritual gifts are presented to you because you now have a higher connection to that pure source. Your physical awareness increases, your healing abilities, yes, even your empathy grows. You have the ability to be present in all sorts of situations and not be affected because your higher vibration negates all that doesn't serve the moment.

An empath will find themselves in all sorts of situations – good and not so good – in order to go through the different types of experiences and to gauge how the energy feels in themselves. How one minute they can be feeling on top of the world, and with just a judgment or allowing themselves to be pulled into the drama, they immediately feel awful.

We're not saying that you need to live your life like a robot. As humans, we will feel emotions. What we are saying is: witness how you react to a situation. See what your reaction does to you physically, emotionally. If you find yourself getting swept into a drama, ground out the energy you're feeling so you can maintain your balance. By doing that, you will be adding your higher vibrational energy into the mix and actually changing the energy around you.

A few years ago Alex was helping out in a retail store. He took a phone call from a customer who was very irate. By this time he'd begun to understand how his energy could help or hinder a situation. The more he tried to reason with the customer, the angrier the customer became. He found himself starting to get pulled into the situation, his own anger and frustration rising. Suddenly, he realized what he was doing. He was getting sucked into a me versus the customer scenario. He abruptly stopped and instead mentally pictured his aura filling with love and light. He then pictured his aura lightly encompassing the customer. After a few moments, he was surprised to find the customer calming down and by the end of the phone call, the customer was apologizing to him for being so angry. He saw that this stuff really worked.

He remembered back to those times when he'd been filled with a fear, whether it was a worry, a responsibility, or a particular thought process. His first reaction was to hide because he didn't want to feel the heavy emotions. He tried the protection. But he learned these experiences didn't go away. The more he protected, the more he became a "worthy opponent" and the more these experiences came at him. So his first phase of testing began. The process of being present.

When you allow yourself to be present in energy, you begin to face your fears. These fears can be simple. They can range from being afraid of making a wrong decision to, once the psychic gifts begin to kick in, seeing something that will happen and being unable to change it.

Forgiveness is one of the biggest gifts of an empath. By forgiving, you're no longer attached to the person or the situation. You're lightening up the energy within and without you. By not forgiving, you're denying yourself the opportunity to fully embrace your life. It takes a lot of energy to never let go. To never forgive. You are actually empowering the person who hurt you – you're giving them your power, your energy. We've seen many situations where the person who did the hurting has moved on – is enjoying their life, never giving thought to what they did, while you're still suffering, still angry, no matter how many years have gone by. That's living half a life.

You don't need to forgive the deed. But you can start by forgiving yourself, even if it's simply forgiving yourself for holding on for as long as you have. And if you had absolutely no blame in the situation, you can step back, try to see the person in the bigger picture (what led them to do what they did – was it childhood trauma? Insecurity? Anger issues?) and then forgive them. The important thing is for you to move on with your life because if you don't, you will never be able to grasp happiness or peace of mind. You will continue fighting a battle that will have no end until your own death. You will wake up leaking your energy and go to bed leaking your energy. You will be pouring all that lower vibrational energy into a world that is already overflowing with it.

There's a saying that is used ad nauseum, but is so true: everything happens for a reason.

And, as we've stated ad nauseum in this book, that reason is that a lesson needs to be learned. Until that lesson is learned, you will continue to draw the same situation to yourself over and over again. You will draw people to yourself that will help you learn the lesson. People often ask us: Why do I keep attracting the same type of person?

Not only is it because there's a lesson to be learned, but there's also the fact that like energy attracts like energy. If you haven't worked on your self-esteem issues, you don't think you're worthy. So what kind of person are you going to attract? Someone who doesn't think you're worthy. It's the energy you're putting out there that will determine what type of person you attract to yourself.

If you're continually attracting a partner who cheats, take a look at your own energy first. What is it about you that is attracting that type of partner to you? Do you interpret love as doing for others – I'll do this and they'll love me? Once again, think about the type of person you'll attract to yourself

– someone who is needy that you will always have to be doing things for until you get to a point where you resent it. If you're a "fixer," you'll attract people to you who need to be fixed. Until you fix that issue within yourself, you'll be stuck on the treadmill, making the same choices over and over again. Putting out that lower vibrational energy over and over again. Yet the situation can always be redeemed. The treadmill can grind to a halt. It starts and ends with you.

Know there is no shame in walking away when a situation turns toxic. Because you feel so much, it takes a great deal of courage to realize you no longer wish to be or need to be part of a debilitating circumstance. As we mentioned in a previous chapter, there will be those people you cannot change; you cannot help. All you can do is love them for the difficult journey they chose for themselves and move on. You have your own lessons to learn without taking on someone else's.

Make Peace

As an empath, your most important lesson in life is to make peace with the process. These situations that occur in your life are not meant to set you up against the world, but rather as a way to experience the world and become a higher way of being. The only way this will happen is to experience those things that make you feel uncomfortable. You can then use the tools we've outlined here to get back to that place of inner comfort. You can't run and hide from experiences because you only make the energy worse by putting your lower energy and thoughts into it. You limit the energy coming to you because of your own limited thought process. The method of grounding, not labeling, allowing yourself to be present and witnessing quickly moves uncomfortable energy through your body. This will only happen if you don't perceive the situation as this way or that way. The situation just is what it is. This also helps when you have energy from other people projected at you. By being transparent, those projections from others don't attach to you and dissipate quickly. You don't have self-judgments, self-doubts, nothing dense in your aura that other people's thoughts or feelings can latch onto it. A huge step towards acquiring transparency is forgiving yourself and others. In forgiveness there is no need to be different. You allow yourself to be who you are, just as you allow another to be who they are. You do not attach a chord or anchor to the situation that will only follow you and persecute you. Everything happens for a reason. It's a chance to practice. Without practice, the empath becomes a victim of their experiences. However, with practice, the empath becomes the object of change of their experiences.

11

Energy Evolution

As you learn and surrender to your lessons, your personal vibration and abilities increase. You are evolving to your highest potential and in that evolution are able to help others.

So you've done the work. You've begun the process of healing your fears. You've learned to witness the emotional drama around you and not allow yourself to get sucked into it. You've opened yourself to your guidance and you've begun to see the magic of how manifestation works. You've aligned yourself to your energetic path and your own personal vibration has increased. You've recognized that when you plug into fear, your vibration abruptly goes down and the energy you're feeling starts to feel lousy.

As you go through your life, you understand how freeing it is to actually work on your fears and remove them from your life. You lift a huge weight from your shoulders because you realize that, at the end of the day, it doesn't matter anymore. It does you no good to hold a grudge because you persecute you and your own energy, not the person you're angry at. You learn to forgive because by not forgiving, you carry the burden in your heart and you stop whatever good energy is trying to make its way to you. Once you experience what higher vibrational energy feels like, there is no going back to the way you were. There is a balance, an inner peace that you find that cannot be adequately described with words, but you know it when you feel it.

A word of warning, however. We know many people who become addicted to this higher vibration. They're constantly chasing the next best feeling. What they haven't learned is that we are here on this Earth to live our lives, to experience every single thing that comes our way. Through experience, we learn. But if we are always chasing that spiritual feel-good feeling, we are in danger of missing what's around us. Of simply being and experiencing. We believe that the Universe brings you what you need, without labels, without preconceived notions of what something has to be. We need to trust that what we feel is what we're meant to feel at the moment we're supposed to feel it.

Later on in his life, Alex searched out many spiritual modalities and workshops, always learning, always improving himself. What felt good to him, he incorporated into his "tool box" of knowledge. What didn't feel good, he discarded, yet grateful he'd explored it in the first place, if only to learn it wasn't right for him.

He found a spiritual retreat nestled in the mountains of Maine, surrounded by the lushness of his beloved forests. For the first time in his life, he experienced a week of healthy eating and spending time with like-minded people, learning specific techniques about energy clearing and spiritual cleansing. He was so invigorated, so at peace with himself that as the week drew to a close, he asked himself, why would I ever want to leave this place? I've never felt so wonderful in my whole life.

Yet the day came when he had to leave. On his way home, he drove through a busy, metropolitan city. The week at the retreat had heightened his psychic abilities, as if they'd been fine-tuned to the point of no resistance to what was out there. Stopping at a light, he looked around him, noticing the people on the street going about their daily business. Suddenly, he felt everything they were feeling, knowing everything they were thinking – a kid looking for drugs, a woman wondering how she was going to feed her children, a man terrified he wasn't going to be able to find a job. The more these energies interacted with him, the heavier Alex became. It reached a point where he wanted to scream as these converging emotions threatened to swamp him.

I just can't live in this world anymore, Alex told himself. I have to go back to the retreat. Even if I end up mowing their lawns and washing their dishes, it has to be the best place in the world for an empath to be – the best place for who I am to be.

But rather than turn around, Alex continued on. Reaching the outskirts of the city, he felt that maddening energy dissipate. Calmer in mind and spirit, it occurred to him that he'd felt these kinds of situations before where he'd felt wonderful when he was playing with his energetic modalities, yet crashing when he came back to reality. He pondered this and the answer came to him in a flash of insight.

You cannot practice unless there is a need for a change. At those places where the energy is higher, you can only go as high as the energy that is present. But when you are in places where the energy is low, that is when your true gifts as an empath come in. Your ability to change, your ability to ground, your ability to move the energy. That is what your job is. That is the job of every empath. It is not to hide yourself away, but to learn how to move vibration.

Alex recalled a day not too long before his trip to the retreat where he'd been at work, feeling out of sorts and low. When he finally dragged himself home after a day that seemed to go on forever, he laid down in his bedroom. Immediately, he felt as though someone were sticking a garden hose into his heart. A moment later, his heart began to fill up with a love so exquisite and all-encompassing he thought he would cry.

"Thank you!" he called out. "This is exactly what I needed today."

He continued to lay in bed, feeling this love fill up every nook and cranny of his body. Yet, something was wrong. The love didn't stop flowing into him. He was so filled up, he couldn't take any more of this high vibrational energy. Still it continued. It reached a point where the love was so intense, he felt he would explode.

"Stop!" he screamed.

The energy abruptly ceased. He sat up in bed, shaking from the experience. He then heard a voice say to him, "We cannot put new wine into old skins. We can only put new wine into new skins."

In his quest to figure out his life, Alex had studied the Bible, the Koran, the Torah, and several Eastern religious texts. He knew the words he'd just heard came from the New Testament of the Bible. He'd never really understood the saying before.

Now it made perfect sense.

The new wine, that is the knowledge of what it meant to be an empath, could only be put into a body that had been "made new" by discarding old thought processes that no longer served him and actually limited him. Just as Alex was no longer the teenager who hid from everything, his body was now more open, more accepting of the lessons and gifts that he was acquiring.

Alex thought back to his younger days, when he'd been overwhelmed by negativity or allowed himself to get pulled into places full of drama. He'd grown so much by accepting and learning the lessons that these same situations no longer bothered him. He could now hold the space of non-judgment and love in every circumstance he was put into. Maybe, just maybe, every instance was put into his path on purpose to teach him.

Life is a journey, an opportunity to experience and learn. Life is a growth; it's an evolution. It's a journey where, as the body raises its frequency, its spirit raises its frequency as well and the ability to be in the energy is learned as a tool, not as a hindrance.

If Alex had to do it all over again, he'd do it exactly the same way. The trials, the tribulations, the pain, the anguish, the emotions – all those things that brought him to a place of fear had now become his allies, his strengths, his knowings. He believed that even the religious practices that he'd studied so intently were beginning to make sense to him now – whether it be turn the other cheek, the ability to sit in mindfulness and meditation, the shamanistic beliefs of how nature teaches that when things work in balance everything flows perfectly, or just honoring and worshipping a world that so dearly wants us to understand. These were things that Alex knew were the truths of an empath. He no longer feared walking his journey. He knew his presence was a gift to many others – not from a place of ego, but from a place of energetic understanding. He had evolved into something wonderful, something that was part of the solution, not part of the problem. And what was that problem? The energy that humans put back into the earth.

As an empath, you can take up the mantle of energetic responsibility by presenting yourself as a channel or a light, so that others can experience your energy and learn from that. You are the example to others so they can know they don't need to live their life in constant drama and draining energy. To understand they can make choices to have a better life by looking at their own energy and how they use it. Do they use it to attract something to themselves? To attract people to themselves? A sexual energy to make themselves feel better? The latest car or electronic gadget to fill up a hole within themselves? To feed on other people's energy because they haven't learned the most important lesson in all this – that all energy comes from Source, not from each other.

You've been through the rigors of spiritual boot camp. You've learned to handle any and all types of energy that come at you. You're survived intact and have reached a level of inner peace and understanding of how things work and why they work. You can now turn that understanding to helping those around you become aware of their own energy: how they use and project their energy and how they can heal their dysfunctional energy. You can create a domino effect – helping one person who in turn helps another and so on. It is only by this process that the world can shift into a space where the fear mongering, the selfishness, and all the other lower energies can begin to dissipate, and respect for each other as a fellow traveler in this life can begin to manifest.

It is our belief that empathy is a phenomena that increases with each generation that comes into this world. There is something obviously going on. Many of our children are having trouble getting through each day. Psychologists who work with young children and teenagers are seeing an explosion in their practices of children who are overloading with energy, but have no idea what to do or how to deal with it.

It is our job to ease them into this, to help them understand that empathy is not a curse. That in order to help sweep away all the darkness of the world, we only need to allow our higher vibration to shine.

The Vibration You Send

Be yourself. Empaths spend so much time trying to be the chameleon of each situation in order to fit in and feel comfortable that they begin to lose sight of what's most important. You are here to serve as an example to others. Every interaction with every living thing has an energy. If you react with duality, shutting down or projecting back, is that energy allowed to flow through from a higher source? No. But if you present yourself as open, not labeling, not judging, the energy flows easily. You allow others to be comfortable in your presence. The vibe you send out is one of comfort and safety. Imagine if the world were to start practicing this. How different this earth and our existence would be.

We would also ask that if you feel so intrigued, go back into any of your religious beliefs or even some you may have shunned and pushed away. Look at them from a different perspective – the perspective of an empath who, like many of the masters who have come before us, learned and taught the ability to move and change vibration. If you look at the sacred texts through the eyes of someone who has learned what energy is and how it is used, you'd be amazed at how once misunderstood or vague verses now make sense.

12

We Are a Gift to Each Other

As you evolve, you will learn the gift of service to others who have forgotten their own paths. It is a difficult world out there, but there is a way to get through it. This is the role of the empath: to learn the way and then teach others.

An empath feels and experiences energy in the moment. Your first thought is why and what am I feeling? Your first impulse is to go into the file system in your brain that has recorded every experience you've had so far in your life.

Your experiences are your past.

As soon as you align a feeling with your past, it creates your reality at that moment. Now you're living in the past and the past always has a lesser vibration frequency to it. Using the past experience as a gauge, you think this similar experience is going to be the same as before. By doing that, you have now projected the energy you're feeling into the future. It doesn't matter if the experience you are reliving was good or bad. It's a judgment that is being projected into the future and that energy is always of a lesser frequency because you are putting your will into it.

The trick is to realize you don't know what this experience means at the moment. You just need to be present in this experience to the best of your ability. Not to judge it or manipulate it. And especially not to fear it because that's a learned response from something in your past. Nor to attach a label to it because you really don't know what it's going to be. Simply be present and witness it, because life is constantly changing. What happened in the past doesn't necessarily mean it's going to happen again in the future. Each experience you deem "bad" served as a lesson. Hopefully, you were smart enough to learn from it. And if you did learn from it, you can in turn help others not to fall into the same energetic traps you did.

Everyone is talking about enlightenment these days. Everyone wants to reach enlightenment. Some don't even quite know what enlightenment is, believing it to be some type of nirvana where you can sit on the couch all day and feel blissful.

True enlightenment is the permission you give yourself to live life. To experience how things feel to you.

Life isn't about perfection and feeling good all the time. It's about being here in all this crazy energy and experiencing it all and being okay with it all. Because, heaven forbid, you're supposed to experience something that's scary that will get you to the next level, but because you believe you're supposed to be feeling good all the time and refuse to look at the creepy crawly things beneath your own rock, you miss that lesson and you don't progress to the next level. There are so many people in the New Age community who believe that all you need is a crystal, or a talisman or some outward item that will protect you and keep you happy so you don't need to do the inner work. But that's all an illusion. In essence, they have created a false god and have given over their own power to this false god. Yes, a crystal or a talisman or a healing can open the window and get a person to feel something they've never felt before. However, the high energy these people feel doesn't last because it isn't real and they're condemned to constantly be chasing it, or going repeatedly to healers who only offer band-aids. You'll walk out feeling pretty good, but how long will it last? If you haven't dealt with your core issues, you'll be back in the dumps before too long and the lesson will play itself over and over again until it is learned.

If there is one thing an empath learns, it's that objects hold energy. But the energy in the object is only as strong as what has been projected into it. High vibrational energy flowing through an individual is where true healing takes place. Shamanic cultures call this becoming the hollow bone – the healer basically gets out of the way and allows the vibration of the universe to flow through them into the client. By getting out of the way, where their thoughts or physical experiences don't dictate where the energy will go, it allows that higher source to direct where the energy is needed most. The energy stays in its pure form, without labels, without judgments, without duality, without human-led direction. The energy now flows from a place of perfection. In that space, true healing can take place.

As an empath and as a human being, who are we to judge another person's path? All you can do, who has done your own work and achieved a high vibration, is to allow the individual to feel that high vibrational energy. To experience your light. Who knows? By doing that, you may be helping that person see their destiny, discover their own path. But if you judge, instead of giving them good energy, you are giving the person you are judging lower vibrational energy that doesn't feel good. And the dysfunctional, negative wheel just keeps turning with nothing changing.

Enlightenment is a balance of the energy of the Universe with the energy of the earth. Perhaps this is what is meant by the saying, "As above, so below"; the ability to channel that which is truth in energy form into the earth plane so that the plan of salvation can unfold. It's the ability to stand in the middle of it all and be okay with whatever you're feeling. To give yourself permission to be life, to try things you might never have tried before because you were afraid of judgment and condemnation. With no harm towards anyone, or coming from a place of ego. To stand in your truth and be all right with that. To be a light and not a judge.

How many bad things in life have happened to teach people wonderful things, allowing them to discover higher strengths within themselves and access incredible knowledge? If we were to judge every feeling or thought that is "bad" in some way, can this be enlightenment? Certainly not from the experiences and knowings of an empath.

Throughout history, spontaneous gifts of knowledge were given when the time was appropriate. Einstein was given the theory of relativity during what he called his thought experiments. He didn't get his theory from a lab. He got it by going within. Many of the greatest composers believed their best compositions were given to them by the angels. Paul McCartney was given the tune to "Yesterday" during the dreamtime.

Is it possible that if we allow ourselves to feel our emotions at any given moment that other gifts of music, or artwork, or profound thoughts will flow into us? As an empath, you are already attuned to the energies around you. If you allow yourself to simply be in the moment, what sorts of thoughts could occur to you? Thoughts that come from a higher source? Thoughts that allow your sixth sense to grow and deepen?

We may not all be Mozart, who was able to write down his great symphonies and operas without one error on the parchment. Yet people like Mozart were able to access higher planes of knowledge when the time was appropriate. We believe empaths have this ability. Once you graduate from spiritual/energy boot camp, without the energetic land mines we as humans set up for ourselves, without the labeling and judgments and plugging in of your own or others' drama, which only hinder the mind, imagine what you are capable of.

The history of spiritual enlightenment itself came through visions to those who transcended these things. They came to a higher knowing. They weren't special. They weren't different from us. We each have the opportunity to reach that place of peace and openness. If I represent myself as open, I grow. My knowledge of love is not from people or even from myself. It just is. All I have to do is allow myself to access it. As the heroes of mythology, who were tested in unimaginable ways, we too are tested. This is the journey of the empath. It isn't easy.

Think of historical figures in the past who had an inkling or a certain knowing of their destiny, yet continued on their path because they knew it was the right thing to do. People like Jesus, Gandhi, Martin Luther King, and Abraham Lincoln, who knew or had a premonition they were going to die, but continued on trying to change the world. They did this because they were able to see the bigger picture. They were the gift to us because despite what they knew could happen to them, by shining their light and walking their path, they gave others options on how they could live their lives. Now obviously, many of us won't be on that grand a stage. Yet, if we are able to change only one life by being that light, we have changed one person's destiny. We have allowed that one person to make a better choice for themselves.

Alex once went to see a renowned spiritual teacher who had written many books and was well-respected around the world. During his speech, the teacher brought up the Garden of Eden. He informed the audience that in the Garden of Eden, humans had everything. They would think of something and it would appear. Flowers, trees, complete bliss-out.

"And you know what happened?" he asked the audience, a twinkle in his eye. "We were bored. There were no challenges, nothing to look forward to, nothing to experience. So we left the Garden by eating the apple. And what did the apple give us? The power to know good and evil. The power of duality. The knowledge that you either have something or you don't. We had everything and now we don't. What did this start? Need, desire, wants. We now spend eternity trying to create our own reality from our perspective of what we think we need or desire or want. Life after life after life, we do this. Even when we get something, it isn't enough. Because we came from perfection. It becomes an addiction. If you think of an energetic frequency as a staircase, each time you learn a lesson and your frequency goes up, it's as if a little bit of our needs have been met and we advance a rung."

There are references in many religious cultures to what we know of as the chakra system. It's a belief that there are energy centers in our physical body, starting at the top of our heads and moving down to the bottom of our feet. Each of these energy centers align to a part of the body and represent a lesson in light. The stairs we spoke about above are these frequencies or centers of light. An an empath, you learn about these centers and experience them with your complete being.

You all start, as Alex did, with the first chakra. Located at the base of your spine, the color of this root chakra is red. It is about survival. How can you survive with these feelings and knowings in your body? How can you get through every day without becoming overwhelmed with all the energy swirling around you? How can you begin to start feeling comfortable in your own skin and not believing you're a freak?

The second chakra, called the sacral, is located below your belly button. Its color is orange. This is your emotional center. Alex's emotional upheavals served to teach him about true emotional energy and how it works.

The third chakra, located above the belly button is your place of will. Its color is yellow. Alex had to learn what "will" truly means. Was it other's wills projected at him or his own will when he changed himself energetically in every situation to feel safe? Was he manifesting from a place of his own will, or from a higher will?

As these three chakras integrated and he learned their lessons, he moved on to the fourth chakra. This is the heart chakra and is located in the center of your chest. Its color is green. This chakra involves lessons of love. Alex now began to embrace his empathic journey. He learned all things happen for a reason. His survival was not something that had to be forced or worried about. The gift of his abilities was his survival. His emotions were not hindrances. They were gifts of feelings and understanding the complexities of this world. He surrendered his will to higher energetic powers. He knew he was led along his path and was gifted, not from a place of aggrandizement or material gain, but from a place of service to everything around him that allowed what he needed to flow towards him. As he learned each lesson of the chakras, he made his way up the staircase towards ascension, one rung at a time. His heart became who he was. He understood the energy that came into him every day was perfect. It was up to him on how to use it.

The fifth chakra, located in the throat, is blue in color. This is the chakra that allowed Alex to speak his truth with love and compassion.

The sixth and seventh chakras are the gateways to ascension and enlightenment. These are the givers of psychic gifts and the connection to Source.

Humanity is now functioning from the first three chakras. You see this when you see the world we've created. A world full of wars, bitter struggles, disrespect for the environment and other living creatures. You can't change the world all at once. But you can change yourself. If each person changed themselves, even a little, imagine how the energy would feel then.

If you're in step with your destiny and are manifesting out of a place of no fear, no ego, the energy feels so pure, so flowing that things manifest much quicker. An empath who has done the work and has reached that place of inner peace is like a little orb of light in a dark world. As an empath, when you are given the opportunity to manifest in connection with your own plan, you serve as a reminder to others. You awaken each other. When you work together, humanity as a race moves into what service is all about. You can't do it without the next person because that person may be the one who helps you figure it out. If you hate them, you lose. If you judge them, you lose.

The heroes in many of our mythological stories and in many of our current movies and books are people who did what they weren't supposed to do. They had to go through many trials and tribulations only to end up back where they started. Yet when they returned, they were not the same people who had started out. They were stronger and wiser. They were now ready to be of service to their community. They were ready to help and to assist others who hadn't gone through what they'd gone through. They were ready to make a difference in the lives of those around them.

Empaths are on a journey to learn autonomy in energy. To learn energy comes from Source, not from each other. To connect with Source and feel the higher vibrational energies of unconditional love. We are gifts to each other. We are the light to others. Yet, like the mythical heroes, you cannot reach the point of being that light unless you too have gone through your own trials and tribulations.

To those of you who hold onto outside items, like crystals, etc., that help you feel better or help you experience an energy, stop for a moment and consider, why am I feeling this? How can I take this feeling and learn from it and keep it going and help others? Yes, the crystals and oils and whatever other items you use can serve as a reminder that there is energy to feel. But ideally, why do you need triggers to feel good anyway? Shouldn't you be feeling this all the time? The energy you feel is within you, not outside of you contained in a tangible object.

The crystals and talismans can help open you up. However, there are still experiences to get through – difficulties that, although hard to undergo, serve their purpose by getting you to the next step of true enlightenment. Part of true enlightenment is not seeing everything as black or white, good or evil. That is the goal of enlightenment – of reaching that space of non-duality and of non-judgment. Things just are. It's the labels we insist on putting on everything that limits our thinking and experiences. Just experiencing things as they come at you allows you to reach that space of inner peace and non-judgment, which allows you to then turn around and help others on their paths. You are the example of a person who has elected to get off the treadmill of seeking validation from others. The true place of validation resides in your own heart and soul. You were created for a purpose. As the example of what can be achieved, you can now bring that light to others, one person at a time.

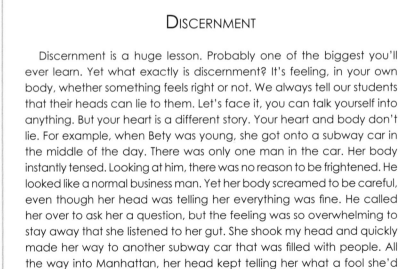

DISCERNMENT

Discernment is a huge lesson. Probably one of the biggest you'll ever learn. Yet what exactly is discernment? It's feeling, in your own body, whether something feels right or not. We always tell our students that their heads can lie to them. Let's face it, you can talk yourself into anything. But your heart is a different story. Your heart and body don't lie. For example, when Bety was young, she got onto a subway car in the middle of the day. There was only one man in the car. Her body instantly tensed. Looking at him, there was no reason to be frightened. He looked like a normal business man. Yet her body screamed to be careful, even though her head was telling her everything was fine. He called her over to ask her a question, but the feeling was so overwhelming to stay away that she listened to her gut. She shook my head and quickly made her way to another subway car that was filled with people. All the way into Manhattan, her head kept telling her what a fool she'd been to be so frightened. All he wanted was to ask directions. It wasn't until a few days later that she heard on the news about a man who had raped a woman in that subway station on the day she'd been there. The description matched the man she'd seen. Now this is a bit dramatic, but it shows how your head can convince you of something while your body is telling you something completely different. This is what discernment is. An empathic person learns at a young age and into adulthood how another person is truly feeling. Not by what they're saying or wearing, but by the energy that is projecting from them. The man on the subway looked normal. Spoke normally. To look at him, you would never know he was a rapist. Yet his energy spoke differently. His energy was the truth of who he was. As an empath, Bety picked up on it. She trusted what she felt in her heart, rather than listen to the logic in her head.

As you learn to discern the different energies of what you're feeling on a daily basis, keep one eye on the bigger picture. If you're a people pleaser, try to fix it by becoming authentic in who you are. The more authentic you become, that is, growing more comfortable in your own skin and accepting your gifts rather than fighting them, the more you give someone else an opportunity to be authentic. How? By putting your own authentic energy into the situation. Doing that allows them to be okay with where they're at and how they feel about themselves. It doesn't always work. Some people simply cannot do the inner work. Yet, if they're willing, you're creating a wonderful place to begin the healing process, both for yourself and the other person.

So the next time you're confronted with a situation that feels off, before you automatically go into your head and try to fit logic to it, just feel it in your heart and in your body. If it doesn't feel right, go with that feeling, no matter what your head or someone else may be telling you. Learn to trust your own instincts. We laughingly call this our "spider sense," but it works. Begin to learn to trust this. It's there for a reason. It's part of learning what the energy of truth feels like.

Afterword

Hopefully, after reading this book, you've come to an understanding that empathy is not something to be feared or hated. There are so many wonderful things that find their way into an empath's life. Just a few include sharpened psychic, healing and precognitive abilities and, the most important gift of all, changing the energy within and without you.

So many people want to change the world. They go to rallies, they walk with placards, they protest, they fill the airwaves and social media with messages of peace and love and understanding. Some turn radical in order to force change. But at the end of the day, nothing ever really changes. People continue their busy lives, immersed in their own personal dramas, struggling with their own personal demons, manipulating, terrorizing, distorting, whether it be the average person on the street or a world leader.

*However, what would be it like if we
lived in a world where everyone was empathic?*

What would it be like if each one of us felt each other's thoughts, feelings, emotions, and choices made throughout the day? In actuality, this isn't that far off. It's happening now as many are beginning to see these kinds of abilities in their children.

As an empath, you experience so much of this in your life. You learn that it is the energy that is most important, not the physicality of the experience.

Maybe this is where it's all going. Maybe to change this world, we need to be in the energy of this world. Only by experiencing this the way the empath does, will enlightenment come to all the craziness that is happening now.

True peace is not being affected by the mess around us. True peace is not hiding away and hoping it all goes away. True peace is in the knowing that *I am the light* and the example that flows through, as so many masters have tried to teach us. Embrace being an empath and know that the gift you are is the solution. By becoming the solution, you can bring change to this world, one person at a time, starting with yourself.